A MATTER OF LIFE

A MATTER OF LIFE

edited by
CLARA URQUHART

LITTLE, BROWN AND COMPANY
Boston   *Toronto*

COPYRIGHT © 1963 BY CLARA URQUHART

ALL RIGHTS RESERVED. NO PART OF THIS BOOK MAY BE REPRODUCED IN ANY FORM WITHOUT PERMISSION IN WRITING FROM THE PUBLISHER, EXCEPT BY A REVIEWER WHO MAY QUOTE BRIEF PASSAGES IN A REVIEW TO BE PRINTED IN A MAGAZINE OR NEWSPAPER.

LIBRARY OF CONGRESS CATALOG CARD NO. 63-13455

FIRST AMERICAN EDITION

PRINTED IN THE UNITED STATES OF AMERICA

For
ENRICO

CONTENTS

INTRODUCTION	9
GÜNTHER ANDERS	15
DAVID BEN GURION	31
ISAIAH BERLIN	39
ROBERT BOLT	43
MARTIN BUBER	51
ALDO CAPITINI	55
LAZARO CARDENAS	65
NORMAN COUSINS	71
DANILO DOLCI	87
ERICH FROMM	97
SHINZO HAMAI	109
EYO ITA	113
KENNETH KAUNDA	125
SALVADOR DE MADARIAGA	141
ODD NANSEN	147
JAWAHARLAL NEHRU	171
SALVATORE QUASIMODO	175
HERBERT READ	179
BERTRAND RUSSELL	189
ALBERT SCHWEITZER	199
MICHAEL SCOTT	209
HANS THIRRING	219
CARL-FRIEDRICH VON WEIZSÄCKER	237

INTRODUCTION

WE are living in an age that involves us all – one with another – in a manner without precedent. The problems that face us are no longer confined to any one land, or to any one form of civilization; and the words of John Donne: 'Any man's *death* diminishes *me*, because I am involved in *Mankind*; And therefore never send to know for whom the *bell* tolls; It tolls for *thee* ... ' have never had the same urgency.

Throughout the ages teachers of morals have taught that ethical principles have meaning only if they are universal. But in practice it has been generally accepted that a personal ethic can never be the same as a social ethic; a national ethic can never be the same as an international one.

Today, however, scientific achievements are slowly making contemporary man aware that some laws must be based on ethical standards instead of on national interest. But this awareness does not come easily. Political opportunism, nationalism, economic factors, tradition, ignorance and apathy, all play their part in hindering awareness of our situation.

While we shall go far astray if we ask only how to prevent nuclear destruction, it is certainly the first step in the direction of seeking an ethical way of life. It is only when enough human beings realize that today the Apocalypse is in the hands of man and not of the gods, that we can begin to think clearly about the moral and physical implications inherent in the present situation. It is known that radioactivity recognizes no national boundaries, but it is not realized to what an extent acceptance of the inevitability of an atomic war has become a state of mind. Nor is it realized to what an extent this factor is contributing to a further breakdown in ethical values. Like strontium 90, the symptoms of this

A MATTER OF LIFE

breakdown in ethical values have spread to most parts of the world; and like strontium 90 they are jeopardizing the future of unborn generations.

The will to survive seems to be growing in the aware minority, and the nuclear disarmament movements are its most apparent symptom. But the will to survive – and in a minority at that – is not enough. If man has a right to survive, he has a duty to survive as a morally whole human being. Civilizations have flourished when the duties and responsibilities of the citizen have been emphasized; they have declined when the notion of rights overshadowed the notion of duties. The signs that the decline in our values is caused at least in part by overemphasis on rights at the expense of obligations are everywhere to be seen. Another factor in this decline is our infatuation with technical and scientific progress, frequently at the expense of regard for the humanities. Benedetto Croce, immediately after the explosion of the atomic bomb on Hiroshima, wrote:

> Scientific discoveries are not the light of truth, that truth which alone enlightens and fortifies, the truth which is good for the soul and which scientists and inventors do not give us, but only geniuses of religion, philosophy and poetry, be they called Jesus of Nazareth, Socrates, Homer, or Shakespeare. Only these are able to make of us true human beings. The discoveries of natural sciences, as Bacon believed, do indeed increase man's command over things, i.e. the power of his hands, but not of his soul. They make the 'animal sapiens' more and more armed with a knowledge which is as vast as it is dangerous. In order to avert this danger and draw from scientific discoveries the good that can be derived from them, there is needed not only a proportionate but a superior advancement of the intellect, of the imagination, of moral faith, of religious spirit; in one word – of the human soul. If this should not come about, it would be

INTRODUCTION

better if the disintegration of the atom, like the treasure of the Nibelungen, be submerged in the Rhine (or perhaps in the Mississippi) and that nations should compete in vain to recover it.

Human intellect, imagination and spirit lag far behind scientific advancement. Many laws, for example, are practically and morally obsolete in view of the present world situation. On an international plane some progress was made at the Nuremberg trials. There it was agreed that obedience to unethical laws was judicially and morally wrong. At his trial Adolf Eichmann pleaded: 'It was not I who persecuted the Jews; this was done by the government. I accuse the rulers of abusing my obedience. Obedience has always been praised as a virtue.' But obedience without consent – the consent of conscience – can never be a virtue. Conversely, disobedience – to be acceptable – must be based on an ethical approach to life.

While there is now a special urgency about the moral issue of when and when not to obey the laws of one's land, this is a question that has been posed throughout the ages. The early Christian martyrs, for instance, could not find it in their hearts to obey the laws of the Romans, and so complete was their inability to do so that they preferred to be thrown to the lions. Later they were sanctified. Had it not been for them and others like them who found courage to face death or isolation rather than to obey when their consciences bade them do otherwise, we would still, metaphorically speaking, be living in caves. In such men we have the true heroes of the human race.

It would seem that in the industrial age it has become harder for a human being to hear the voice of his own conscience. Primarily this is so because he leads an extroverted life, and has been unable to achieve the inner progress needed if he is to survive morally in the machine age. And it is in this no-man's-land between his obsolete inner organization and the new ethical evolution not yet achieved that man's destructive instincts are capable of creating physical and moral havoc too frightful to envisage. With all his talk of freedom, modern man has become a conformist as never before. How then can ethics play a significant role in his life? Conscience, by its very nature, is non-conformist; it has to be capable of saying no when all the others are saying yes. It has to be without doubts as to the ethical basis on which the refusal to comply is based. The more conformist a person is, the less is he able to hear the voice of his conscience, or, if he hears it, to obey it.

And yet a small number of modern men, aware of the dangers that threaten us, are manifesting not only the will to survive, but the will to find a cure for the moral sickness of which the nuclear danger is but the most frightening symptom. Among them are those who do not know what is to be done; who feel inadequate and confused. It is my hope that the thinking of the people who have contributed to this book will make aware those who are not yet aware, and help those who, while aware, are still bewildered.

London CLARA URQUHART
January 1963

GÜNTHER ANDERS

Dr Günther Anders was born in Breslau in 1902 and received his Ph.D. in 1926. He is a professional philosopher, critic and translator. From 1933 to 1950 he lived in France and America. In 1950 he settled in Vienna. His study of Hiroshima, *Der Mann auf der Brücke*, published in 1958, won the Italian prize Omega.

1. *Hiroshima as World Condition*

ON August 6, 1945, the day of Hiroshima, a new age began: the age in which at any given moment we are able to transform any given place on our planet, and even our planet itself, into a Hiroshima. Since that day we have become (at least *modo negativo*) omnipotent; since, on the other hand, we also can be wiped out at any moment, we have also become totally impotent. However long this age may last, even if it should last for ever, it is the Last Age, for there is no possibility that its *differentia specifica*, the possibility of our self-extermination, can ever end – but by the end itself.

2. *The Time of the End Versus the End of Time*

Thus, by its nature, this age is a 'respite'; and our 'mode of being' in this age cannot be defined but as 'not yet being non-existing', 'not quite yet being non-existing'. Therefore the basic moral question of former times has to be radically reformulated. Instead of asking: '*How* should we live?' we now have to ask: '*Will* we live?' And for us, who are 'not yet non-existing' in this Age of Respite, there is but one answer to this 'How?' Although at any moment the time of the end could turn into the end of time, we have to do everything in our power to make the end time endless. Since we believe in the possibility of the 'end of time', we are apocalyptics, but since we fight against the man-made apocalypse, we are – and this has never existed before – 'anti-apocalyptics'.

3. *Not Atomic Weapons in the Political Situation, but Political Actions in the Atomic Situation*

Although sounding absolutely plausible, it is misleading to say that there exist atomic weapons in our political situation. This statement has to be turned upside-down in order to become true. As the situation today is determined and defined exclusively by the existence of atomic weapons, we have to state: political actions and developments are taking place within the atomic situation.

4. *Not Weapon, but Enemy*

What we are fighting is not this or that enemy, who could be attacked or liquidated by atomic means, but the atomic situation as such. Since this enemy is the enemy of all people, those who, up to now, had considered each other to be enemies, have now to become allies against the common menace. Peace actions from which we exclude those with whom we wish to live in peace amount to hypocrisy, self-righteousness and a waste of time.

5. *To Threaten with Atomic Weapons is Totalitarian*

A pet theory, broad enough to be embraced by subtle philosophers, as well as brutal politicians, by Jaspers as well as by Strauss, runs: 'If it were not for our ability to threaten with total annihilation, we would be unable to hold the totalitarian menace in check.' This is a sham argument for the following reasons: the atom bomb has been used, although those who used it were not in danger of falling victim to a totalitarian power; this argument is a fossil from the 'ancient' days of atomic monopoly and has become suicidal today; the catchword 'totalitarian' is taken from a political situation which not only has already fundamentally changed, but will continue to change – atomic war, on the other hand, excludes all chance of such a change; by threatening with atomic war, thus with liquidation, we cannot help being totalitarian. For this threat amounts to blackmail, and transforms our globe into one vast concentration camp, from which there is no way out. Whoever bases the legitimacy of this extreme deprivation of freedom upon the alleged interests of freedom is a hypocrite.

6. *Expansion of our Horizon*

As radioactive clouds do not bother about milestones, national boundaries or curtains, distances are abolished. Thus in the 'time of the end' everybody is in deadly reach of everybody else. If we do not wish to lag behind the effects of our products – which would be not only a deadly shame but a shameful death – we have to try to widen our horizon of responsibility till it equals that horizon within which we can destroy everything and everybody and be destroyed by everybody – in short, till it becomes global. Any distinction between near and far, neighbours and foreigners, has become invalid; today there are only *proximi*.

7. *The United Generations*

It is not only the horizon of space which needs to be widened, but also that of time. Since acts committed today (test explosions, for instance) affect future generations just as perniciously as our own, the future belongs in the scope of our present. 'The future has already begun', has always already begun, since tomorrow's thunder belongs to today's lightning. The distinction between the generation of today and that of tomorrow has become meaningless; we can even speak of a League of Generations to which our grandchildren belong just as automatically as we ourselves. They are our 'neighbours in time'. By setting fire to our houses, we cannot help making the flames leap over to the premises of the future, and the as not yet built homes of the as yet unborn generations will fall to ashes, together with our own homes. Even our ancestors are fully-fledged members of this League. For by dying, we would make them die, too – a second time, so to speak – and after this second death, everything would be as if they had never been.

8. *Nothingness – the Effect of the Not-Imagined Nothingness*

The apocalyptic danger is all the more menacing as we are unable to picture the immensity of such a catastrophe. It is difficult enough to visualize someone as not-being, a beloved friend as dead; compared, however, with the task our fantasy has to fulfil now, it is child's play. For what we have to visualize today is not the not-being of something particular within a framework, the existence of which can be taken for granted – but the non-existence of this framework itself, of the world as a whole, at least of mankind. This 'total abstraction' (which, as a mental performance, would correspond to our performance of total destruction) surpasses the capacity of our natural powers of imagination: '*Transcendence of the Negative*'. But since, as *homines fabri*, we are capable of actually producing nothingness, we cannot resign ourselves to the fact of our limited capacity of imagination. The attempt, at least, has to be made to visualize nothingness.

9. *We are Inverted Utopians*

The basic dilemma of our age: 'We are smaller than ourselves', incapable of making a picture of what we ourselves have made. Therefore we could call ourselves 'inverted Utopians'. While ordinary Utopians are unable to actually produce what they are able to visualize, we are unable to visualize what we are actually producing.

10. *The Promethean Discrepancy*

This 'inverted Utopianism' is not simply one fact among

others, but the outstanding one, for it defines the moral situation of man today. The dualism to which we are sentenced is no longer that of spirit against flesh, or of duty against inclination, is neither Christian nor Kantian, but that of our capacity of production as opposed to our powers of imagination.

11. *The Supra-liminal*

It is not only imagination which has ceased to fall in line with production, the same lack of co-ordination has befallen feeling and responsibility. It may still be possible to imagine or to repent the murdering of one's fellow man, or even to shoulder the responsibility for it; but to picture the liquidation of one hundred thousand of our fellow men, this definitely surpasses our power of imagination. The greater the possible effect of our actions, the less we are able to visualize it, to repent it, or to feel responsible for it; the wider the gap, the weaker the brake-mechanism. To do away with one hundred thousand people simply by pressing a button is incomparably easier than to slay one individual. The 'sub-liminal' (the stimulus too small to produce any reaction) is well known in psychology; more important, however, though never seen, let alone analysed, is the 'supra-liminal'; the stimulus too big to produce any reaction or to activate any brake-mechanism.

12. *Senses Distort Sense – Fantasy is Realistic*

As our pragmatic life horizon (the one within which we can reach and be reached) has become limitless, we must try to visualize its character, although by trying this we would evidently violate the 'natural narrowness' of our imagination. Although insufficient by its very nature, besides imagination there is nothing which could be considered as an organon of truth. Certainly not perception. It is a 'false witness', in a far more radical sense than Greek philosophy had meant when warning against it. For the senses are myopic, their horizon is 'senselessly' narrow. It is not the wide land of imagination in which escapists of today like to hide, but the ivory tower of perception.

13. *The Courage to Fear*

When speaking of 'imagination of nothingness', the act meant is not identical with what psychology imagines to be imagination, for I speak of *fear*, which *is* 'imagination of nothingness', *in concreto*. Therefore we can improve the formulations of the last paragraphs by saying: 'It is our capacity to fear which is too small and which does not correspond to the magnitude of today's danger.' As a matter of fact, nothing is more deceitful than to say: 'We live in the Age of Anxiety anyway.' This slogan is not a statement but a tool manufactured by the fellow travellers of those who wish to prevent us becoming really afraid, who are afraid that we may once produce the fear commensurate to the magnitude of the real danger. On the contrary, we are living in the Age of Inability to Fear. Our imperative: expand the capacity of your imagination, means *in concreto*, increase your capacity to fear. Therefore, don't fear fear itself, have the courage to be frightened, and to frighten others too. Frighten thy neighbour as thyself. This fear, of course, must be of a special kind: a fearless fear, since it excludes fearing those who might deride us as cowards; a stirring fear, since it should drive us into the streets instead of under cover; a loving fear, not fear of the dangers ahead but for the generations to come.

14. *Productive Frustration*

Time and again our effort to comply with the imperative (widen your capacity to fear and make it commensurate with the immensity of the effects of your actions) will be frustrated. It is even possible that our efforts will make no progress whatsoever, but even this failure should not intimidate us. The repeated frustration does not refute the need for repeating the effort. On the contrary, every new failure bears fruit, for it makes us vigilant against our further causing effects which transcend our capacity to fear.

15. *Displaced Distance*

If we combine our statement about the end of distances with that about discrepancy – and only this combination makes the picture of our situation complete – we reach the following result: the 'abolition' of time and space distances does not amount to the abolition of distances altogether; for today we are confronted with the daily increasing distance between production and imagination.

16. *End of the Comparative*

Our products and their effects surpass not only the maximum size of what we are able to visualize or to feel, but even the size of what we are able to use. It is common knowledge that our production and supply often exceed our demand and produce the need for the production of new needs and new demands. But this is not all: today we have reached the situation in which products are manufactured which simply contradict the very concept of need, products which simply *cannot* be needed; which are too big in an absolute sense. In this stage our own products are being domesticated as if they were forces of nature. Today's efforts to produce so-called 'clean weapons' are attempts of a unique type; for what man is trying here is to increase the quality of his products by decreasing their effect.

If the number and the possible performance of the already existing stock of weapons are sufficient to reach the absurd aim of the annihilation of mankind, then today's increase of production is even more absurd and proves that the producers don't understand at all what they are actually doing. The comparative, the principle of progress and competition, has lost its sense. *Death is the boundary line of the comparative. One cannot be deader than dead, and one cannot be made deader than dead!*

17. *Appeal to Competence Proves Moral Incompetence*

We have no reason to presuppose (as for instance Jaspers does) that those in power are more able to imagine the immensity of the danger and that they realize the imperatives of the atomic age better than we ordinary *morituri*. This presupposition is even irresponsible. And it would be far more justified to suspect them of having not even the slightest inkling of what is at stake. Only think of Adenauer who dared to berate eighteen of the greatest physicists of today and to tell them that they are incompetent in the 'field of atomic armament and atomic weapons questions', and that they should instead talk shop and not 'meddle' with those issues. It is precisely by using those vocables that he and his kind demonstrate their moral incompetence. For there is no more final and no more fatal proof of moral blindness than to deal with the apocalypse as if it were a 'special field' and to believe that rank is identical with the monopoly to decide the 'to be or not to be' of mankind. Some of those who stress competence are doing it solely to disguise the anti-democratic elements of their monopoly. By no means should we be taken in by this camouflage. After all, we are living in allegedly democratic states. If the word 'democracy' has any sense at all, then it means that precisely the province beyond our professional competence should concern us, that we are not only entitled, but obliged – not as specialists, but as citizens and human beings – to participate in deciding about the affairs of the *res publica*. Since, after all, we are the *res publica*, the reproach that we are 'meddling' amounts to the ridiculous accusation that we are interfering with our own business. There has never been and will never be an affair more *publica* than today's decision about our survival. By renouncing 'interference', we not only fail in fulfilling our democratic duties, but we risk our collective suicide.

18. *Abolition of 'Action'*

The possible annihilation of mankind seems to be an 'action'. Therefore those who contribute to it seem to be 'acting'. They are not. Why not?

Because there is hardly anything left which, by a behaviourist, could be classified as acting. For activities which formerly had taken place as actions, and were meant and understood as such by the acting subjects themselves, now have been replaced by other variants of activity: by working; by 'triggering'.

Work: substitute for action. Already the employees in Hitler's death factories had, so to speak, 'done nothing', had thought that they had done nothing, because they had done 'nothing but their work'. By 'nothing but work', I mean that kind of performance (generally considered to be the only and natural type of operation today) in which the *eidos* of the end-product remains invisible to the operator, no, doesn't even matter to him, no, is not even supposed to matter to him, no, ultimately is not even permitted to matter to him. Typical for today's work: it seemingly remains morally neutral, *non olet;* NO END PRODUCT, however evil, can defile the worker. Nearly all jobs assigned to and performed by man today are assimilated to this universally accepted and monocratic type of operation. Work – the camouflage form of action. This camouflage exempts even the mass murderer from his guilt, since, according to today's standards, the worker is not only 'freed' from responsibility for his work but he simply *cannot* be made guilty by his work.

Consequently, once we have realized that today's fatal

equation runs, 'All action is work', we have to have the courage to invert it and to formulate, 'All work is action'.

'Triggering': substitute for work. What is true of work applies even more to 'triggering', for in triggering the specific character of work, effort and consciousness of effort, are diminished, if not nullified. Triggering – the camouflage form of work. As a matter of fact, there exists hardly anything today which cannot be achieved through triggering. It can even happen that one first push of a button sets in motion a whole chain of secondary triggerings – till the end-result, never intended, never imagined by the first button-pusher, will result in millions of corpses. Seen behaviouristically, such a manipulation could be considered neither work nor action. Although seemingly no one would have done anything, this 'doing nothing' would actually produce annihilation and nothingness. No button-pusher (if such a minimum-operator is still required at all) feels that he is acting. And since the scene of the act and the scene of the suffering no longer coincide, since cause and effect are torn apart, no one can perceive what he is doing. 'Schizotopia' by analogy with schizophrenia.

Evident again: only he who continuously tries to visualize the effect of his actions, however far away in space or in time the scene of their effects may be, has the chance of truth; perception falls short.

This variant of camouflage is unique. While formerly it had always been the aim of camouflaging to prevent the prospective victim from recognizing the danger, or to protect the doer from the enemy, now camouflaging is meant to prevent the doer himself from recognizing what he is doing. Therefore, the doer is also a victim today. Eatherly, who dropped the bomb on Hiroshima, belongs to those whom he has destroyed.

19. *The Deceitful Form of Today's Lie*

The camouflage examples teach us something about the

present-day type of lie. For today the lie no longer needs to couch itself in the costume of an assertion, ideologies are no longer required. Victorious today is that type of lie which prevents us from even suspecting that it could be a lie; and this victory became possible because today lying no longer needs to assume the disguise of assertions. For while so far, in 'honest hypocrisy', lies had pretended to be truths, they now are camouflaging themselves in a completely different costume.

Instead of appearing in the form of assertions, they now appear in that of naked individual words which, although seemingly saying nothing, secretly already contain their deceitful predicate. Example: since the term 'atomic weapon' makes us believe that what it designates may be classified as a weapon, it already is an assertion, and as such is a lie.

Instead of appearing in the form of false assertions, they appear in that of falsified reality. Example: once an action appears in the disguise of 'work', its action-character becomes invisible; and this so much so that it no longer reveals, not even to the doer himself, that ultimately he is acting; and thus the worker, although working conscientiously, enjoys the chance of renouncing conscience with a clear conscience.

Instead of appearing in the form of false assertions, lies appear in that of things. In the last example, it is still man who is active, although he misinterprets his acting as working. But even this minimum can disappear – and this, the supreme triumph of lying, has already begun. For during the last decade action has shifted (of course through human action) from the province of man to another region – to that of machines and instruments. These have become, so to speak, 'incarnated' or 'reified actions'. Example: through the mere fact of its existence, the atom bomb is an uninterrupted blackmailing – and that blackmailing has to be classified as an 'action' is, after all, indisputable. Since this shift of our activities and responsibilities to the sphere of our products has taken place, we believe we will be able to keep our hands clean, to remain 'decent people'. But it is, of course, just this abdication of responsibility that is the climax of irresponsibility.

This, then, is our absurd situation: in the very moment in which we have become capable of the most monstrous action – the destruction of the world – actions seem to have disappeared. Since the mere existence of our products already proves to be action, the question of deterrents is an almost fraudulent one, since it obscures the fact that the products by their mere existence have already acted.

20. *Not Reification but Pseudo-Personalization*

One wouldn't exhaust the phenomenon by labelling it with the Marxian category 'reification', for this term designates exclusively the fact that man is reduced to a thing-function. We are stressing, however, the fact that the qualities and function taken away from man by his reification are now becoming qualities and functions of the products themselves, that they transform themselves into pseudo-persons, since, through their mere existence, they are acting. This second phenomenon has been ignored by philosophy, although it is impossible to understand our situation without seeing both sides of the process simultaneously.

21. *The Maxims of Pseudo-Persons*

These pseudo-persons have rigid principles of their own. The principle of 'atomic weapons', for example, is pure nihilism, because if they could speak they would say: 'Whatever we destroy, it is all the same to us.' In them nihilism has reached its climax and has become naked *Annihilism*.

Since action has shifted from man to work and products, examination of our conscience today cannot confine itself to listening to the voice of our own heart. It is far more important to listen to the mute voice of our products in order to know their principles and maxims – in other words: the 'shift' has to be reversed and revoked. Therefore, today's imperative runs: *Have and use only those things, the inherent maxims of which could become your own maxims and thus the maxims of a general law.*

22. *Macabre Abolition of Hatred*

If the scene of action and the scene of suffering are torn apart; if the suffering does not occur at the place, or the act; if acting becomes acting without visible effect, suffering becomes suffering without identifiable cause, hatred disappears, although in a totally delusive way.

Atomic war will be waged with less hatred than any war before. Attacker and victim will not hate each other, since they will not even see each other. There is nothing more macabre than this disappearance of hatred which, of course, has nothing to do with peacefulness or love. It is striking how rarely Hiroshima victims mention those who have caused their suffering, and with how little hatred they do it. This, however, does not mean that hatred will play no part in the next war. As it will be considered indispensable for psychological warfare, the production of hatred will no doubt be organized. In order to nourish what a perverted age calls 'morale', identifiable and visible objects of hatred will be exhibited, in emergency cases invented – 'Jews' of all kinds. Since hatred can bloom only if the objects of hatred are visible and can fall into the hater's hands, it will be on the domestic scene that one will choose scapegoats. Since the target of this artificially manufactured hatred and the target of the military attacks will be totally different, the war mentality will become actually schizophrenic.

Whatever I may have dictated here, it has been said in order not to become true. If we do not stubbornly keep in mind how probable the disaster is and if we do not act accordingly, we will not be able to prevent the warnings from becoming true. There is nothing more frightful than to be right. And if some among you, paralysed by the gloomy likelihood of the catastrophe, should already have lost his courage, he too still has the chance to prove his love of mankind by heeding the cynical maxim: 'Let's go on working as though we had the right to hope. Our despair is none of our business.'

[Translated by the author]

DAVID BEN GURION

David Ben Gurion was born in Plonsk in 1886. He was one of the organizers of the Jewish Labour Party in Israel, and from 1921 to 1935 Secretary General of the Federation of Trade Unions.

Following the United Nations Partition Resolution in 1947, he was elected National Chairman in charge of Security and Defence. He was Prime Minister and Minister of Defence in the provisional government, and in the Government of Israel from 1949 to 1953. In 1953 he resigned, but has been Prime Minister and Minister of Defence since November 1955 with only brief intervals.

Over two thousand seven hundred and fifty years ago two of Israel's prophets, Isaiah and Micah, prophesied total disarmament, the abolition of armies, and the abandonment of all warfare and military training.

> And it shall come to pass in the end of days [said Isaiah] that the mountain of the Lord's House shall be established at the top of the mountains, and shall be exalted above the hills; and all nations shall flow unto it. And many peoples shall go and say: 'Come ye, and let us go up to the Mountain of the Lord, to the House of the God of Jacob; and he will teach us his ways, and we will walk in his paths.' For out of Zion shall go forth the Law, and the word of the Lord from Jerusalem. And He shall judge between the nations and shall decide for many peoples; and they shall beat their swords into ploughshares, and their spears into pruning hooks; nation shall not lift up sword against nation, neither shall they learn war any more. (Isaiah ii. 2–4.)

And Micah added:

> But they shall sit every man under his vine and under his fig tree; and none shall make them afraid; for the mouth of the Lord of Hosts hath spoken. (Micah iv. 4.)

In other words, perfect and universal security will reign, and men shall do their work in peace and quiet, without fear or anxiety, and enjoy the fruits of their labours.

Unlike the sages of other nations, including Plato, who saw the Golden Age in the distant past, the prophets of Israel envisaged international peace and happiness in the future, far away in 'the latter days'.

In our day, the aspiration for disarmament and the

A MATTER OF LIFE

safeguarding of international peace has become humanity's most vital and urgent problem.

Is there a short and easy way to the solution of the problem? Is it merely a question of the individual conscience? Is individual disobedience enough?

The prophets of Israel were not mystics, and did not seek salvation for themselves alone. They were men of vision, they saw deep into the profundities of man's being, his needs, his fundamental characteristics. They combined the vision of 'the City of Righteousness, the Faithful City' (Isaiah i. 26) with that of the Redeemer, who 'shall judge the poor with righteousness, and decide with equity for the meek of the land ... for the earth shall be full of the knowledge of the Lord, as the waters cover the sea.' (Isaiah xi. 4, 9.) Their vision of the future, therefore, was not meant for a select few, but for all mankind.

Today, almost three millennia later, we are living under very different conditions. The world of Israel's prophets was confined to the nations of the Middle East and the Eastern Basin of the Mediterranean; they knew almost nothing of the peoples beyond – either Western or Northern Europe, the wide expanses of Eastern Asia, the African Continent beyond the Nile Valley, or of course America and Australia. But although our world has grown and expanded since then, yet in effect distances have been shortened today; and the great continents and oceans have shrunk, as it were, thanks to modern means of transport and communications. In our day it is easy to contact the other end of the world, and an event anywhere on earth becomes known almost in the twinkling of an eye all over the globe. Never was the entire human race so closely interconnected as it is today, and any local dispute – Congo, the Berlin problem, the strife in Laos, Indonesia's claim to Dutch New Guinea – immediately becomes a world problem. Needless to say, the dangers now in store from a world war are infinitely graver and more deadly than all the conflicts of the ancient days, or even the two world wars of the first half of our century.

DAVID BEN GURION

The 'Cold War', which followed the second World War, is now the main source of fear and anxiety, for even the man in the street is aware of the appalling destructive weapons at the disposal of the two mighty powers facing each other across the barricades: the Soviet Union and the United States.

About two years ago Mr Khrushchev submitted to the United Nations Assembly a disarmament plan that might almost have been copied word for word – though in somewhat more modern style – from the prophecies of Isaiah and Micah. There were many who doubted the sincerity of the proposer and the seriousness of his proposals. These doubts grew after the multi-megaton atomic bomb tests conducted by the Russians one after the other, and the threats uttered from time to time by the Chiefs of the Soviet Army. The author has no doubt whatever of the Russian people's wish for peace, as he has no doubt of the sincerely peaceful desires of the American and European peoples.

In spite of the gap in time that divides us from the era of Isaiah and Micah, it seems to the author that the prophets' way to peace between the nations – the establishment of 'the City of Righteousness' – is still the right way. Today, however, this means not the *polis*, the individual city, or even the individual state, but entire continents. The difficult and critical problem of our day, which may well endanger the peace of the entire world, is not the ideological struggle between the democratic West and the communist East, but the gap – material and cultural, economic and educational – between the nations that won their independence during the post-war period – primitive, impoverished peoples, ridden by disease and ignorance – and the wealthy, highly developed and flourishing nations of Europe – both East and West – and North America.

Civil disobedience might perhaps satisfy the individual, who separates himself from society and his environment, and quiets his conscience, but this personal avenue of escape which the individual might find for himself will solve no problem.

A MATTER OF LIFE

If mankind is indeed doomed to nuclear war, what advantage is there in the segregation of a select few who refuse to soil their fingers with this dangerous weapon? The multi-megaton bomb will not distinguish between the righteous and the wicked, the infant and the greybeard. They need no mass armies to work them; only a few airmen, or submarine pilots, or highly skilled mechanics, to press the button somewhere or other, that sends off the missiles with their nuclear warheads, or shoots down high-flying aircraft, the bombs that can destroy at one stroke the greatest cities, entire regions with millions of people.

I have no definite knowledge of Dr Schweitzer's aims in going to live in the jungle to establish a hospital in an area of darkest Africa. But it seems to me that he showed the right method or, perhaps, rather the right direction, towards a solution of the supreme problem of our day. World peace will be ensured if the right way is found to close the gap between backward, poor, diseased and illiterate countries in Africa, Asia, and Latin America, and the progressive, wealthy countries richly endowed with health and skills, in Europe, North America and Australia.

As for Communist China, her plans and intentions for the future are not clear, though she plainly does not welcome with enthusiasm the Soviet Union's watchword of coexistence.

China is the most populous country in the world, containing some quarter of the human race, but whatever her intentions may be, if Asia (beyond the borders of China and her satellites in Mongolia, North Korea and North Vietnam), Africa, America, Europe and Australia succeed in establishing in their midst 'the City of Righteousness' whose strength rests on the foundation of the utmost co-operation and equality in cultural and economic values and assets, the world will be redeemed from the nightmare of destructive war, and international peace will be secure. The problem that confronts most of the Latin-American peoples, almost all the peoples of black Africa, and the greater part of

Asia, is not the choice of political régime, but development, the education and health of the people, and the gradual raising of the living standards of the masses, to the level of Europe, Australia and North America.

It is for all the civilized nations of the world to work for the solution of *this* problem – and here there is also room for the activities of individuals, following in the footsteps of Dr Schweitzer.

The real content of the 'Cold War' is the struggle for the souls of the peoples of Asia, Africa and Latin America, and there can be no more effective, dedicated and practical contribution to world peace than material and cultural assistance to the backward peoples in wiping out their poverty, disease and illiteracy. This aid should not be extended as a matter of charity or philanthropy, but as the duty of one member of the family of man to his fellows, without arrogance or boasting, but out of a pure and profound feeling of human love, in the consciousness that the full participation of all nations in the values and assets of the civilized states is as necessary for the developed peoples as for the backward ones. The European nations, which for decades and centuries ruled over weaker and poorer peoples, owe a great debt to those who have at last won freedom from the foreign yoke.

But independence is not enough. For centuries the foreign ruler has deprived the subordinate peoples of the benefits of science and technology and growing control over nature and its resources. The oppressed peoples must be given back their rights; that means, full equality in health, education, know-how and economic development. The new nations should be assisted by their richer neighbours on this earth out of a sense of duty, in profound humility, in the conviction that all men have a common destiny, and must enjoy real and full equality.

The intellectual leaders of all nations should show a personal example in the giving of this aid, which aims simply at enabling the underprivileged nations to help themselves.

ISAIAH BERLIN

Sir Isaiah Berlin was born in 1909 and educated at St Paul's School and Corpus Christi, Oxford. He was Lecturer in Philosophy at New College in 1932, and a Fellow of New College from 1938 to 1950. Since 1957 he has been Chichele Professor of Social and Political Theory at Oxford.

EVEN though all institutions are means to the goals that men pursue for their own sakes and not ends in themselves, yet some of these, like language, family, and other forms of basic social intercourse, are part of the essence of what men are and cannot be donned and doffed like a cloak. And since these essential institutions require rules and at times authority to enforce these rules, if men are not to collide with each other and suffer too much, this is the case for authority even on utilitarian grounds. For this reason I agree with Hume, that stability in a society is important, so that it may be better at times to suffer bad laws than to alter these laws so frequently as to undermine the authority of laws and institutions as such, which may end by causing greater misery than the bad laws and institutions themselves. But peace and stability – still less laws, customs, rules – are not an ultimate value, as are truth, or love, or friendship, or freedom, or art, or justice, or equality, or life itself.

Every man carries within him some image or notion more or less clear, of what human beings are, and therefore what actions will diminish or destroy the minimum degree of humanity without which men cannot live as men. If I am ordered by an authority which I normally accept, whether on conscious utilitarian grounds, or as part of my normal habits of life (and such acceptance comes to involve a good deal of faith, loyalty, and emotional attachment), to do something that goes against this basic concept of man, I am morally entitled to resist.

Indeed, this is what morality is about. Where passive disobedience should turn into active resistance – even terrorism – will depend on how high a price I think it right to pay to hamper or destroy such authority. If it is such that I believe that no worse rule could exist, and that the consequences of its destruction cannot possibly be worse than its retention, that no other methods likely to remove such rule are open to me, and that the act of disobedience is likely to help to alter the situation for the better, I am forced to extreme measures. But unless I have rational grounds for thinking all this, my resistance is not justified.

If I accepted Lord Russell's argument during the first World War, or believed what he believes about nuclear war today, I should like to think that I should behave like him. But in fact I do not agree with his premisses or conclusions in either case.

ROBERT BOLT

Robert Bolt was born in 1924 and educated at Manchester Grammar School. He attended Manchester and Exeter Universities and has been an English teacher. His plays, which have achieved world fame, include *Flowering Cherry*, *A Man For All Seasons*, and *The Tiger and the Horse*.

THE kind of disobedience practised by nuclear disarmers has been non-violent civil disobedience. Non-violence forbids either damage to property or the use of physical force. This seems appropriate. Nevertheless, civil disobedience entails a definite breach of the law. Is the campaign therefore revolutionary?

A thief commits a crime because he wants money. If he could, he would prefer to lay his hands on it without crossing the police. His breach of the law is incidental to his purpose. In contrast, the purpose of civil disobedience in breaking the law is merely that: to break the law. When nuclear disarmers sit down in the road, it is not that they desire to stop the traffic and this the most effective way they can conceive of doing it. (On the contrary, the free flow of traffic is neither here nor there to their intention, and in any case this a very inefficient means of stopping it.) It is simply that this is a fairly harmless but flagrant crime. They cross the police not incidentally but of set intention. A theft is an attack on constituted society but only, as it were, in passing. A sit-down is an attack on constituted society and deliberate.

To that extent the civil disobedience campaign for nuclear disarmament cannot escape from being revolutionary.

But it is unlike any usual revolutionary movement.

In the first place, it has no programme for altering society. Its single purpose is to stop the making or holding of nuclear weapons, by any government, in any country, on any pretext. If this purpose were achieved I am inclined to think a new kind of society would result, but that is nothing to the purposes of this campaign.

In the second place, if it is to be effective it must be, if not strictly democratic, at least very popular. A small number of people throwing plastic bombs expresses its opinion very effectively. A small number of people sitting in the road is simply silly. It needs thousands (I would say it needs hundreds of thousands) of people sitting in the road to be effective. In this campaign sheer numbers are what count and the contribution which the most distinguished individual makes is identical with that made by the most anonymous: the addition of one unit.

And it is to the individual and the individual conscience that the appeal of the campaign is addressed. What is more, it is addressed not to the revolutionary, either by conviction or temperament, but to the law-abiding, to those with a stake in ordered society – to the father and mother, for example. When such people break the law, even in a token manner, they make a small sacrifice in comfort, a considerable sacrifice in personal dignity, and a great sacrifice in peace of mind. But the nuclear war towards which the world is drifting would destroy society and with it the dignity of the individual which is a social product. And so it is not in opposition to decency and good order, but in the name of decency and good order, that such people make this sacrifice. The more law-abiding, the greater their sacrifice and the greater the degree of moral suasion they bring to bear upon their fellow citizens. Conversely, the less the less, and the less their action need be heeded.

It is the whole of humanity that is threatened with disaster, not this or that section of it. And we are threatened, not because of wicked or wickedly incompetent statesmen on this or that side of the Iron Curtain, but because we are all helplessly caught up in attitudes of national interest, national hate, above all national fear, which simply are not adequate to our actual situation. Neither the Eastern nor the Western bloc positively wants to use these weapons; each is prepared to from fear of the other. Fear makes us dangerous and danger increases our fear. And as fear and danger circle together we see that the leaders of East and West whirl one another nearer to the brink with each new crisis. There is not an individual on the surface of the globe who wants it. There is not an individual anywhere who is not sickened at the mere prospect of it. Yet we prepare and draw towards it as though we were compelled.

The national statesmen cannot break the circle because their mandate is to act in the national interest. Only the private individual can act in the name of humanity; the lead must come from below.

And the lead must come in a form so definite and vigorous that statesmen can see that a new force has been placed at their disposal, and a new mandate given them. That is the justification on non-violent civil disobedience.

To break the law of the land is always serious, but it is not always wrong. There is some mystery here, because there is no law behind the law by which we may judge the law. (Unless you are lucky enough to believe in God's law and believe that you know it.) Nevertheless, we do judge the law. When we hear, for example, of Nazi laws authorizing the murder of Jews, we do not say: 'That was the law of the land, so it must have been right.' We say: 'That was the law of the land, but it was wicked; it was not only the right, but the duty of the ordinary, decent citizen to break it whenever he could.'

Some who agree thus far object that Nazi states are totalitarian, whereas we live in a democracy. So long as we have the free vote, they argue, we have no right to break the democratically enacted law.

Myself, I find this a very strong argument, but not final. It is not impossible for a democratically elected government to enact wicked laws, even as wicked as the anti-Semitic laws of the Nazis. (It was indeed the democratic vote which first raised the Nazis to power.) And suppose yourself to be living under such a government. Suppose you found yourself by chance in a position to release a wagon-load of Jewish children on their way to some English Auschwitz, say while the policeman's back was turned. Would you really think it right to refrain from that unlawful act and wait for the next election?

A MATTER OF LIFE

Then am I really suggesting that the evil of merely possessing the Bomb, which is at worst a merely incipient evil, is comparable with the actual evil of Auschwitz?

No, of course not. But just this is the point: once Auschwitz was in operation the time for resistance was past, because the penalty for resistance then was to go into Auschwitz yourself, your wife and children too. No one can hold the German people guilty for their failure to resist under those circumstances, for only saints and heroes could have undertaken it. It was earlier, when the Nazis were strong but not yet irresistible, when the evil was not yet actual but only incipient, it was then that the ordinary German citizen incurred his guilt, by placing his comfort, his everyday dignity and peace of mind before his plain duty to resist. And that is our case now. It will be too late to protest when the bombs are falling, and the evil our society has accepted is no longer incipient, but actual. If we fail to resist, effectively, now, while we can, we shall be responsible and for an evil compared with which the sufferings endured in Auschwitz will seem trivial.

It is not surprising that the first substantial protests should be made in liberal democracies where the democratic liberties obtain. I think the movement will spread; I hope it will become world-wide. But this much is certain: it is no act of God or nature which threatens us, but we ourselves. The Bomb has no volition of its own. If we use it, it can only be because we choose to, because mankind is a species which – let him explain it how he will – would, on balance, rather die than live. Would rather die, that is, than find the courage to abandon ancient attitudes and the energy to find new ones. I do not believe that this is so. I believe – with an effort I believe – that ordinary individuals have the will to live and the courage and the energy. If that is so they have only to express it.

Mankind is moving towards death as a sandhill moves, not by any sinister mechanism it contains but by the shifting of its myriad tiny grains in one direction. The campaign of civil disobedience is no device to force it backwards. It simply asks any individual who may be listening to move, himself only, in the opposite direction. And this is not arrogance surely, but humility to accept the tininess of your own importance and rely on that. In any case, for the ordinary individual nothing more is possible. I don't think anything less will be effective.

Certainly I don't believe it possible to work out any system of diplomatic checks and military balances which will make us safe. No device, no arrangement can henceforth make man anything less than terribly dangerous. His only safeguard is his attitude to himself. If he will have mercy on himself then the terrible danger becomes a marvellous potency. This is not merely visionary, it is merely practical. All men *are* brothers now. We may be brothers in life or brothers in death, as we choose, but brothers we shall be. The situation is too novel for prediction, we cannot know where the new road will lead. But the old one is leading unmistakably towards the cliff's edge and the only place to start a journey, long or short, is wherever you happen to be standing. We happen to be standing here.

But why civil disobedience? Why not the safer, more dignified, traditional methods? The situation isn't either safe or dignified and can't be. It is lethally dangerous, and primitive. Neither is it traditional, but new. The diplomats are in conference again, struggling hard by the old methods; and getting the old answer. The growing indignation, dwindling hope, mounting conviction that the other side means ill, exhaustion among the statesmen, creeping passivity among the people, increasing deference to the military man and his requirements – how often have we seen it all before?

The old answer in the new situation means death. We need a new answer. The statesmen need a new impulse and a new mandate. There is just a chance that this unsafe, undignified but new method of civil disobedience may give it to them.

But having said all that, I know that this argument, carried to its conclusion, would lead to chaos. I know that society is a shelter we do well to remain in and do well not to tamper with. Happier generations than our own have lived whole lives within it. But moments can arise when the individual is made to realize that society is *only* a shelter and that finally he is alone, on the surface of the planet, with a decision to make. I believe we may be living at such a moment.

MARTIN BUBER

Professor Martin Buber was born in Vienna in 1878. He holds honorary doctorates in law, divinity and letters, and is Professor Emeritus of Social Philosophy at the Hebrew University in Jerusalem. Among his better known publications are: *I and Thou*, 1937, *Between Man and Man*, 1947, and *Images of Good and Evil*, 1952. Together with Franz Rosenzweig he translated the Bible into German. He has written many works on Hasidism and Zionism.

I AM constantly being asked how civil disobedience can legitimately be justified, not in a given historical situation but quite generally. In general terms, I know no other answer than that disobedience of this nature is legitimate when it is in fact obedience, obedience to a law superior to that which is being disobeyed here and now – in a word, when it is obedience to the supreme law. Here I am faced with a new question – how do I know what the supreme law commands for the present situation? In the language of the Gospel parable: where is the limit to that which I must render unto Caesar?

Every attempt to answer this question on a general level in terms of unassailable validity must be doomed to failure. In our world, the absolute in the field of politics cannot prove its indisputable superiority over all things relative; the self-appointed representatives of the absolute know fairly well how to use dialectics to denounce the disobedient.

Every Caesar, every empire, no matter what form these may assume, every historically established power appears to its subjects to exist by the grace of God, no matter what name that God may have.

Thus we are ultimately driven to abandon the examination of this issue in general terms, and to make it plain beyond all doubt that this question must be considered within the context of the given situation. It is not my task to state where what I consider legitimate disobedience begins for all times and for all circumstances, but where it begins here and now.

In the circumstances in which we live, it has become simpler to state this than at any previous time in the history of mankind.

For through his own actions, man is on the point of permitting his participation in the shaping of his destiny to slip through his fingers. Those who are undertaking the all-out military preparations of today refuse to recognize what these very preparations may entail. There is the possibility that in the course of the warlike competition between the two adversaries – while apparently everything is in the hands of man as before – the most dangerous of our products will take the ultimate step and succeed in reducing the human cosmos to a chaos beyond our imagination.

Are the masters of the moment in a position to call a halt to the process, over which they merely appear to have control? Will they still be able to avoid a war waged with the ultimate means of destruction? In other words – instead of talking at cross purposes of fictions called 'politics', will they ever learn to talk to each other of reality, that is to say, to clarify the interests common to both sides as well as those that are conflicting, and as a result of this reach the conclusions which every independent thinking individual has already arrived at today? Should the masters of the hour, as I suspect, be unable to do this, then who is there to fill the breach if not those who by their civil disobedience pit themselves against the erring powers? Surely a world-wide front of those who practise civil disobedience must stand at the ready, prepared not for battle but for the redeeming dialogue. Who are these individuals, if not precisely those who hear a voice calling to them from out of the present situation, this situation of human crisis, and who obey that voice?

ALDO CAPITINI

Professor Aldo Capitini was born at Perugia in 1899 and received his M.A. in philosophy and literature at Pisa. In 1933 he was dismissed as Assistente to the University for refusing membership of the Fascist Party. During this period he published two books on the lines of Gandhi's teachings, *Elementi di Un' Esperienza Religiosa*, and *Vita Religiosa*. Imprisoned in 1952, he organized the Centre of Social Reorientation upon his liberation. From 1946 to 1956 he instructed at the University of Pisa in pedagogy, the history of religions, and moral philosophy. Since 1956 he has taught at the University of Cagliari.

i

IT is evident that the development of modern ethics has, for centuries, been in two directions: the affirmation of the value of inwardness, of the supreme decision of the conscience of the individual; and the widening of moral interest to all rational beings as persons who merit equal rights.

Both these directions have illustrated the struggle to deny absolute values to ecclesiastical or state institutions; to refuse commands with constricting effects issued by such institutions; to oppose conformity with, and obedience to, laws and customs for the sole reason that they are traditional; and to overcome the eternal division of the human race into the saved and the damned.

And while the one direction has been building up an ever more universal concept *of law*, that is, such as to be valid for all (Kant), the other direction has been aiming at building up a universal concept *of fact*, diffusing civilization to all beings, in a cosmopolitanism which is moving towards horizons hitherto unknown.

ii

Probing deeper into this matter, it is found that in 'inwardness' of conscience the individual has found a reason for opposing the absolutism of tradition and the past, and the enlightening confidence of having reached maturity, and of 'daring to know and to think'; but that a later drama was shaping itself, that of the first and second halves of the eighteenth century: the struggle between an ethical institutionalism (Hegel) which puts the substance itself of the individual in an intricately woven institutional canvas, such as family, society, and state, and the forces to be liberated from every institutional and intimately collective canvas making appeal to God (Kierkegaard) or affirming will to power (Nietzsche). This labour has lasted some decades and has produced grave crises. At the present time, in a horizon ever more clearly world-wide, two directions are making themselves evident, and these are: on the one hand, placing greater value on society than on the state, bringing a solid international organization into being; and, on the other, the mutual existence of all beings in the act and method of non-violence.

iii

In this movement of moral ideas and forces, how does the problem of obedience fit in, that is, the problem of the conflict between liberty and authority? The transcendent foundation of authority has obviously been in a state of crisis for centuries. Where does a command for imposing itself upon us as absolute find its justification? Nations subjected to adverse weather conditions may find a sign of authority for the 'commandments' in thunderbolts, that is, in the capacity to put those disobeying the commandments to death. But can power or threats produce obedience in a conscience which seeks rather to be convinced? Faced with a commandment based on power, individuals either obey hypocritically without waiting for true conviction, or else seek to placate the Almighty with cult and superstition because He can change wrath into pardon or into smiles. Or they may begin subtle rationalization for evading the law in the name of special motives, with all the fastidious work of casuistry. The point is often reached where the absolute commandment is subjected to so many exceptions that it is no longer possible to see where the absolutism is. It would have been better to say that morality is a creation – a serious creation – of the conscience, rather than to present a commandment as if issued by absolute authority, for example, that of 'thou shalt not kill', and then to disobey it a thousand times. If the authority is absolute, this, therefore, entails uneasiness in disobedience. It is better to put things in another way. It is not on account of the king that there are citizens; at the most they are 'subjects'; but it is on account of the citizens and their liberty, that authority exists.

iv

This is, in fact, the work done by centuries to present the law in a manner different from the authoritative, absolute, institutional manner of tradition. The law to which we give our obedience is that of which we are convinced: we acquire such conviction by the exercise of reason and experience. For example, solidarity with all rational beings is reconquered, not by a command founded on authority, but by an accumulation of motives of dialogue, of opening, of growth of our being. When we have to act we do not ask what absolute command exists which is appropriate to the case, but we question tradition, which is a store of long historical experience, we examine the situation, and we consider that which every other rational being should do in our place; we put together various elements to produce our action, or those laws or directive principles which concern groups of actions. In this way our actions are creative, our obedience is persuaded.

v

This method of proceeding stands up well to the accusation of being rebellious, or selfish, or disorderly. First of all it is easy to point out that everyone does *actually* act in this way, that is, only obeys laws to which he, with his own hands, has opened the door of his own conscience. There is only this difference: that some choose an authority, and thereafter are disposed to obey every command which that authority may issue; others, on the other hand, often prefer to re-examine the reasons for the commands and give no one the key to their own consciences. This does not mean that for every decision, for every law, for every regulation, they must make a deep study, but the fact is that they recognize no authority, not even the government of their country, or the president of their society, as being absolute, that is, subject to no control. This second method will be more laborious, but it is certain that the first is highly dangerous, because the habit of questioning is lost, and it is bad for him who exercises power, and for him who is under its exercise.

vi

The best rule is that in our actions (obedient or disobedient) we should establish a habit, custom, or method, which is their *raison d'être*. It is true that we consult our consciences, but a long education in the appreciation of values (arts, sciences, honesty, liberty, charity) makes our consciences more apt to decide well. It also helps to think that our action is valid for all, so that anyone in our place should act in the same way, that we would explain to others what we are doing with the probability of convincing them that it is right, and also to think that all are present and see our every action, even if we are alone. This constant reference to all is to a supreme aid for deciding well, and is also the preparation for that religious sentiment of the presence together of all beings, through which when we choose well (the value) we have the intimate aid and companionship of all.

vii

The conclusion of what precedes is that in the field of ethics, it is necessary to guard oneself against the accusation of 'disobedience', by examining and taking care of ourselves if we are suffering from Pharisaism. Unceasing attention should be turned to the actions of others by trying to individualize in them the creative aspect, the contribution to good, the opening out to greater value, the courage of having decided against the majority. It seems that he who makes himself the instrument of prejudices and privileges contributes little to moral life, whereas, on the contrary, he who tries to awaken the conscience of all, even by his own sacrifice, contributes much. For this reason, to begin with the education of young people, it is good to educate by open dialogue, by listening and speaking, by the loyalty of nonfalsehood, and by the disposition of *opposing*, because in society there are many things still wrong which must be combated and corrected.

viii

I do not believe that the Socrates of Plato's *Crito* is right. This position is prior to Christianity, which has shown in a luminous manner (at least through Jesus Christ) what are the limits of the state. The citizen creates every day his collaboration or non-collaboration with the laws. If he opposes himself to the laws and explains the reasons for his opposition, he also aids those who make the laws, because he induces them to make them better. Only thus can society develop and improve. Citizens should feel that their obedience or disobedience is not a private act, but a public one, in the interests of all, and which will be widely made known. The liberty of association and of expression is the first right of citizens, because it is the method of learning and teaching. Through the liberty of association and expression we have the instruments of power, because power is not only represented by government. For this reason, when a government removes the liberty of association and expression (and it is difficult to find a government which makes such liberty possible and concrete for all) there are strong reasons for being on one's guard and for not conceding obedience at once.

ix

I believe that the problem within present national societies – none of which can give a full guarantee today – should be faced not with a preliminary negation. The disposition towards the national society of which we are part can well be generically favourable through those goods, advantages, values, and instruments of life, which it offers us, and because solidarity between citizens and nationals of the same country is a concrete training for wider solidarity. But, together with this favourable disposition, we should have within us the knowledge that the present laws are, as a whole, somewhat limited, and that there is always the necessity for integration and correction. And this attention to the possibility of changes applies above all in relation to the most important things. Citizens often use the contrary method: disobedience to unimportant laws, obedience to important ones. They have not extended their understanding to seeing that the latter above all are sometimes impositions. Disobedience then becomes an act of bearing witness, as in the shining example of Antigone.

x

We have a decisive case today in the choice between obedience and disobedience, because there is the atomic arms race which could lead to the most terrible war ever known, and to the reduction of Europe to the level of a fallen Greece. Perhaps never as today 'to disobey' is to obey everything; that which is and will be in the universal conscience; to disobey neighbours in order to obey those far off; to disobey written laws in order to obey unwritten laws for being united with all beings; to disobey the cult of present powers in the name of the community which will tomorrow truly be the community of all people. The objection of conscience, by individual affirmation of one's own independence in the face of the serious law to 'kill' human beings, becomes today a warning to all of the terrible danger of atomic destruction. And this is precisely an example of a form of disobedience which seems to be individual, and becomes therefore a priceless asset for all. Perhaps never as at the present time has the world needed the 'coming together' of individuals and of groups who affirm the most valid principles of the written laws. And in the presence of great powers and of politico-military blocs directed by a few people who have the destiny of hundreds of millions in their hands, it is good to affirm on behalf of centres in all parts of the world – numerous as the stars in the sky – the principle of non-violence to unite ever more closely, as never before.

LAZARO CARDENAS

General Lazaro Cardenas was born in 1895 at Jiquilpan de Juarez, Michoacan, Mexico, and educated in his native village. He joined the Constitutionalist Revolution in 1913 and from 1920 to 1921 was Military Commandant and Provisional Governor of Michoacan, and Constitutional Governor of Michoacan from 1928 to 1932. In 1933 he became Minister of War. From 1934 until 1940 he was Constitutional President of the Republic. In March 1961 he presided over the Latin American Conference of National Sovereignty, Economic Emancipation and Peace, in Mexico, and at the present time is part of the Collective Presidency of the World Council for Peace.

DISOBEDIENCE, or in more familiar terms, resistance to injury or the threat of injury, cannot be thought of as negative, whether in the relationships of individuals or societies. Known as disobedience, collective resistance could be an act of affirmation, of faith in human and social integration.

Man, in his long and eventful history, has sought and found his own unbroken way to progress, by drawing on his relationship with his fellow men. For reasons now abundantly obvious, it has not always been easy and peaceful. These reasons would be the same in conflicts which might come in the future as they were in the past, however transformed in appearance: social inequality has lasted from remote times until the present day. The unavoidable consequence of the inequitable contract between individuals and between nations is the struggle between groups developing a nation, and later the struggle between nations already evolved.

Disobedience derives from these disputes, being the passive or active resistance of one part of a society to the other. The moral and ethical quality of disobedience depends upon the proportion of individuals or groups physically or morally injured by the remainder. If the victim is the majority, disobedience is rooted positively – it has justice as its base.

In reality, human societies developed in the pattern of obedience to minorities who monopolized material wealth, and, consequently, civil, military and religious power. Modern societies, built upon the great popular revolutions in the last two centuries, which succeeded in sweeping away the anachronisms hindering material and intellectual advance, achieved a high standard of economic and political organization, proclaiming a democracy which in the event has been more abstract than real. Some societies having continued in the way of oligarchy, great majorities have been compelled to disobedience, and resistance to injustice. Today, separate upheavals have established a perspective of justice for entire peoples. Society as a whole is demanding, for its logical development, new ways of living together, true universal democracy, peace among independent nations, and social justice for all men.

Thus, in conditions obtaining in the world as we know it, the disparities between one section of society and another have become more obvious. Knowledge of the causes enables us to predict with some exactness what general pattern will be adopted by disobedience, or the resistance of the great human majorities who for centuries have suffered from inequalities.

The roots of the theory of disobedience go right down into the past, as far as the first primitive executive authority. In the social and political development of peoples the theory has played a dynamic role, being responsible for the great revolutionary transformations. Furthermore, the vital seed was introduced into two crucial documents which enshrined the principles of the first revolutions of modern times, and which opened the way to those of this century. Thus the Declaration of Independence of the United States proclaimed in 1776 that: 'All men are born equal; that they are endowed by their Creator with certain inalienable rights, among them life, liberty and desire for happiness.' In the Declaration of the Rights of Man and of the Citizen it is clearly affirmed that: 'The object of all political society is the protection of the natural and ineluctable rights of man; these rights are liberty, security and resistance to oppression.' Both imply the right of disobedience before the threat of a violation of the natural rights of man.

Today disobedience takes on a universal value as the highest moral and ethical expression of the general resistance to the use, and even the existence, of weapons capable of destroying man and his heritage of civilization and culture.

The urgent need to protect the human species from the dangers of nuclear war obliges us to concentrate and redouble our efforts to close the fissure which has been opened by nuclear tests. Already through it are penetrating the first dangers to the physical and moral health of all peoples. The sinister effects of radioactivity in the atmosphere and on the ground, following the experimental explosions, will, according to the anxious studies of eminent scientists, not only harm the present generation, but seriously threaten the health of those to come.

I have said before, and say again now, that the responsibility for this problem of peace and war falls upon the great nuclear powers, and they too must decide whether further tests shall be carried out. No nation has the right to impose upon another a destiny not of its choosing. Here it is fitting to quote the great humanist Albert Schweitzer, who said:

> Until now it has not been remembered that the question of whether or not tests should be continued is something which concerns not only the countries producing nuclear weapons, about which they make arbitrary decisions. Who authorizes these powerful nations to carry out experiments which may result in grave harm to all countries? What of the rights of peoples, sung so much in our time by the United Nations?

Among the peoples of Latin America, and I believe also among the greater number of African and Asiatic peoples, the area in which disobedience will be practised, in its profoundest and most ancient sense, will be that sector of society where their normal development is most harmed, and their material and spiritual interests most aggrieved. The methods of resistance, determined by actual conditions prevailing in each country, may vary, but the fundamental content and objective of resistance will in all three continents be the same and, in the last analysis, relate in brotherhood with those of all the peoples of the world. Before social injustice, in a perspective where death leans over life, disobedience is universal.

The prevalence of imperialism, systematic exploitation of foreign countries and peoples—the prime cause of world wars—is the reason for our Latin American resistance. This translates itself into a struggle for the total liberation of our peoples, the swiftest method by which we shall be able to assure our sovereignty and the independence of our countries. Through this we hope to contribute in the most efficient way, and with the help of other peoples, to a world peace which shall be permanent.

I would agree with an eminent Mexican internationalist who declared in the common meeting ground of the United Nations:

> Atomic and hydrogen bombs seem to have cleared away for ever the old concept of victor and vanquished; uniting inextricably all potential enemies in one common destiny – to live or die together.

I would add that this choice is in the hands of the peoples, those who by disobedience in whichsoever of its many forms, must impose their will to live with social justice, nationally independent and in peace.

NORMAN COUSINS

Norman Cousins was born in 1912. He was President of the United World Federation from 1952 to 1954, Vice-President of the American P.E.N. from 1952 to 1955, and holds various honorary degrees. His journalistic awards include the Benjamin Franklin Award for Public Service in Journalism, and his educational awards include the John Dewey Award for Education. He is the editor of the *Saturday Review*.

The question in today's world is no longer pacifism *v.* militarism, or the assertions of conscience *v.* the calculus of nuclear power. The question is, simply, what will work? What will enable this planet to remain reasonably congenial to life in human form? What will enable the human species to grow, evolve, enjoy and justify freedom, and develop the uniqueness that is, after all, the main obligation of organized society to protect?

If modern power, which is to say, nuclear force, could serve these basic purposes, then that would be the strongest case for it. If it could protect a nation against predatory aggression, then it would have an achievable purpose and should be considered in that light. But if nuclear force cannot do any of these things, then the gravest penalty will be attached to the failure to comprehend this fact and act on it. For it would mean that the human community would be staking its life on an illusion instead of mobilizing its intelligence and imagination in devising an effective alternative to force.

The reason modern warfare cannot accomplish the traditional functions of military power is that it has a built-in self-destructive component. It is like a double-barrelled gun, one barrel of which is pointed at the enemy while the other is pointed squarely at the head of the man about to shoot. No truth in the modern world is more difficult to comprehend and act upon than that nuclear warfare is a supreme form of collective suicide. It will not save the lives, values, or properties of the nations involved; it will neither yield the benefits of victory nor avert the catastrophe of defeat.

Conventional ideas of defending the homeland and preserving its values are meaningless. Of all the implications of atomic energy, none is more basic than this. And that is why the theory of the deterrent offers no reasonable hope of protecting a nation, its people, its freedoms.

A MATTER OF LIFE

It may be argued that, mutually destructive though atomic weapons may be, they serve to deter an aggressor. At the heart of the deterrent theory, of course, is the belief that a potential enemy will be disinclined to attack if he knows the counter-attack will be immediate and devastating. Advocates of the deterrent idea also contend that the nation's military potential must in no way be modified or hindered by agreements on arms control, or disarmament. Similarly, they regard any security activities of a world organization that impinge upon a nation's freedom of action in the field of arms and power as undesirable. Thus, restrictions on nuclear testing or the development of missiles are generally considered inconsistent with the requirements of a nation's security.

The main flaw in the deterrent theory, however, is that it does not deter. The possession by the United States and the Soviet Union of advanced nuclear weapons has not served as a deterrent to either nation in matters involving their national interests. Neither has allowed fear of nuclear weapons to deter it from making clear that it was prepared to fight with everything it had to keep from being pushed out of Berlin. Each has attempted to convince the other that it is prepared to let fly with everything it owns rather than back down.

It is natural for a nation to display, not restraint, but willingness to march to the brink when its national interests are threatened. Even when the threat is not a major one, there is a natural concern lest an unchallenged small threat lead to a larger one. In a world of anarchy, not deterrents but the compulsions of national sovereignty are the prime movers.

The announcement by one nation that it has achieved a military break-through in one field creates in the other nation not a mood of defeat but a blistering determination to match that particular weapon and surpass it. The United States possessed an atomic monopoly from 1945 to 1948. This period of monopoly coincided with the period of maximum

Soviet aggressiveness and intransigence. Similarly, the advent of the Soviet sputnik, with its portents of long-range rockets carrying nuclear bombs, did not cause the United States to close the gap.

One nation's deterrent becomes the other nation's incentive. The spiralling competition for military advantage carries with it ascending and accelerating tensions. Fear of surprise attack is the greatest single factor in the thinking and planning of the opposing military strategists. The pressure is building up in each country to hit first rather than wait to be hit. The same logic that gave birth to the around-the-clock jet bomber and the nuclear-cocked satellite will argue that there is no choice except to take the final initiative. Thus, the deterrent leads to preventive or pre-emptive war. Since the opposing countries have to contend with the same factors in surprise nuclear attack, each knows the other is considering the same antidotes; the very fact that each is even considering preventive war causes the other to move in that direction itself.

The incredible paradox is that both potential foes today seek security in the same terms. Each calls upon the other to be deterred by its striking power, yet both are becoming more insecure in direct proportion to the increase in their own power.

The theory of the deterrent marks the ultimate failure of unfettered national determination in an internationally anarchic world. Never in history has the sovereign state been more powerful or less secure. Its capacity for waging war has never been so great, nor its ability to protect itself so puny. In turning to the theory of the deterrent for protection, it invokes irrational force as the principal means of creating rational restraint. Far from inspiring great restraints, the deterrent produces jitters and hair triggers.

To return to our central thesis:

What has changed? Not the aggressive habit of nations. This habit persists in intensified force. The danger that a powerful nation may extend its dominion is just as potent as it has ever been. Indeed, this time the entire world, and not just a single state, is vulnerable.

The problem of coping with aggression, therefore, has not changed. What has changed is that the traditional means of resisting aggression no longer works. Nuclear weapons impose a penalty for use just as severe as military disaster. All strategy, military or otherwise, must therefore be turned towards the defence of a nation and its vital interests without precipitating a situation in which nuclear force will be used. The failure of national policy occurs at precisely the point that the nuclear borderline is crossed.

Here we come to a perilous dilemma. A nation may be mindful of the cataclysmic nature of nuclear force. It may be fully aware of the consequences to itself of a nuclear war. Yet it does not wish the potential enemy to take advantage of this fact by undertaking aggressions that might be resisted otherwise. And so a nation feels compelled to assert that it will not hesitate to engage in nuclear warfare in defence of its vital interests. Similarly, the opposing nation feels compelled to assert its own readiness to pursue objectives without fear of nuclear consequences.

The result is that nuclear weapons, far from bringing about a change in the traditional habit of warfare, actually increase the danger of war by fortifying the ultimatum psychology and accelerating the tensions issuing therefrom.

The modern state, therefore, lives on two conflicting planes. On one plane, it must live with the fact of war, as it has done throughout history. It must cope with all the traditional problems and threats affecting its security. On the second plane, the state must live with a totally new dimension in warfare that makes war itself obsolete as the means of defending a nation's security or achieving its objectives. The gap between these two planes represents the vital area that needs to be charted and understood if a nation is to define a workable foreign policy.

NORMAN COUSINS

The security and freedom of peoples are directly tied to the need to create a workable alternative to nuclear force.

The problem seems insuperable until we realize that it can be put in a different form, namely: Is there any way out of the present world anarchy? For it is the lack of law in the international arena that exposes nations to aggression, creates the basic conditions of insecurity, and makes it necessary for a nation to attempt to develop its armaments.

A world rule of law is therefore the only possible answer to the dilemma of international insecurity in an age of nuclear weapons. It is the only possible alternative to the now obsolete concept of force as the means of defending a nation against predatory attack.

What kind of world organization or authority is required for the establishment and operation of a world rule of law? Certainly not a super-state. That would only serve to transfer the force to a monolithic political unit. But a federated world organization, with powers confined to the common security of the nations – such an organization offers substantial hope of avoiding either the slavery of submission or the suicide of nuclear war. Authority adequate to underwrite national independence, to define and carry out a programme of orderly and enforceable disarmament under proper safeguards, to create and co-ordinate a programme for development of resources, especially in those areas most in need of such development – such authority represents the principal functions of an organization aimed at instituting a rule of law in the world.

How should such an organization be created? Is it necessary to jettison the United Nations and start anew? No. The United Nations is the essential and inevitable beginning of what can ultimately become a structured peace. This means the extension of specific machinery for enacting, enforcing, and interpreting world law. The U.N. already exists. It functions surprisingly well in a large number of ways. Despite the veto in the Security Council and the voting structure of the General Assembly, the U.N. has been able to sustain the peace, however precariously, where the vital interests of the major powers are not fundamentally involved. Moreover, the United Nations Charter (Articles 108 and 109) provides the orderly means whereby the United Nations can be changed and strengthened. In particular, these articles anticipate the need for a Revision Conference.

Such a Revision Conference would have to consider present structural weaknesses in the U.N. One weakness, of course, is represented by the veto provision in the Security Council that prevents that body from functioning properly in any threat to the peace involving a major nation. Next is the one-nation-one-vote method of representation in the General Assembly under which several nations with a combined population of perhaps twenty millions of people could outvote a population of two hundred millions.

Fundamentally, of course, the basic purpose of a review conference would be to explore the means by which the United Nations could enact, enforce, and interpret the rule of law. The conference could offer the world a chance to wipe the slate clean. The benefits of participation in such a strengthened body should be equally available to all. Membership should be universal. Any nation sincerely interested in security and the common welfare of the world's peoples should have no hesitation in joining with the rest.

The conditions for membership should be clearly stated: respect for the rights of individual members, prompt fulfilment of obligations, recognition that the human community has precedence over the national community in those specific matters related to a common world security.

The United Nations is not a country club or a fraternal order. It should exist for the purpose of defining the obligations of nations and enforcing them. The more recalcitrant a nation, the more of a problem it represents to world order, the greater the need to have it within the jurisdiction of an ordered world. But universal membership in a U.N. also presupposes responsible authority on those matters affecting the peace.

The aim of a revised U.N., then, would be to have its own actual and potential forces large enough to prevent aggression, or to cope with it instantly if it should occur. It should be able to legislate effectively in the matter of national armaments; which is to say, the world's peoples must have confidence in the disarmament arrangements. It should enjoy the right of inspection to guard against secret manufacture of weapons adapted to mass destruction.

What sovereign rights ought the nations to retain? The individual nations have a right to insist on recapturing sovereignty over their own institutions and cultures. I use the word 'recapturing' because sovereignty in domestic matters has been seriously weakened under world anarchy, with war or the fear of war determining the careers and destinies of millions of citizens, the size of their taxes, or the pressures upon free institutions.

A workable disarmament plan should call for control of all weapons adapted to mass destruction. Inspections and sanctions are mandatory to keep nations from engaging in such manufacture. Atomic energy, for example, should be developed under proper safeguards, with each nation participating as its own resources and industrial establishments would permit, and deriving benefits in proportion to the individual contribution to the over-all effort. This would not exclude other states from atomic benefits, particularly where health and economic development are concerned, but it would leave to those states with atomic energy installations the primary rights of development and use for peaceful purposes. The U.N. inspectors would maintain careful safeguards against diversion of such facilities for military purposes. The U.N. would cease to manufacture atomic weapons once universal membership is achieved in the U.N. and the means for preventing war established.

The principal difference between this plan for control of

atomic armaments and earlier proposals is that the U.N. would now be given powers against war itself. Under the Baruch Plan, for example, atomic disarmament was sought without any comparable machinery for dealing with the circumstances which might dictate the use of atomic weapons. No state under the proposed plan could justifiably argue that control of atomic energy was now being pursued in a vacuum, or that there was no agency strong enough to protect it against war and to ensure its rights.

Just as investing the U.N. with appropriate forces of its own is the precondition for any plan for enforceable disarmament, so the need to create a durable structure for carrying out disarmament would raise the question: what about the over-all form of the U.N. itself?

This form is inevitably related to its own powers and limitations. Law begins with the conquest of force. It moves through the agencies of justice and enforcement. It never allows potential violators to become stronger than the machinery to deal with violators. It is in the implementation of this idea that government takes shape. Whether that government is good or bad, whether it is a government in which all men are subject to the laws, including the leaders, or whether it is a government in which the laws serve the purposes of a few men or a man bent on capturing the state and its people – all these questions depend upon the wisdom and courage of the founders, the popular mandate behind them, and their ability to retain the confidence of the world's peoples.

It seems inescapable that the principles of federalism would have to be seriously examined by a review conference if the United Nations is to possess adequate authority in the area of common security, yet also be able to guarantee retention of internal sovereignty to the individual nations. Let us consider the alternatives.

First, a league. A league is a loose organization of states held together by treaty with the individual nations retaining ultimate authority even in armaments, or other matters related to the common security. In view of the failures of leagues throughout history, including the United Nations and the League of Nations itself, it is to be hoped that the delegates would not tempt history further.

Next, a confederation. A confederation is a step beyond a league; that is to say, an attempt is made at a fairly organic relationship among the states and the obligations of all nations are generally fairly well defined. What a confederation lacks, however, is a structural basis for defining obligations or for the adequate enforcement of its own rules. It lacks a common authority transcending national authority in those matters clearly concerned with common dangers and common needs.

Next, a strong central government. It is doubtful whether the historical conditions exist at the moment for a strong central government of the world. Indeed, the easiest way to kill a centralized United Nations is to impose upon it functions and powers far beyond its capacity. A central government taking upon itself all the powers exercised by the individual nations – powers in the fields of taxation, currency, immigration, trade, economic development, mutual security and defence, general welfare, and so forth – would be dealing with such complexities and imponderables as could bring about its possible early collapse. Moreover, the differences in national institutions and cultures might create an almost insurmountable barrier for any government which attempted to maintain jurisdiction over the individual.

This leaves what is probably the soundest and safest approach of all to the revised structure of the U.N., namely, a federation of limited but adequate powers. In such a federation, each nation would retain jurisdiction over its peoples and institutions in all matters except those clearly related to the common security and common development. There would be clear-cut distinctions between world jurisdiction and national jurisdiction, between the sovereignty that would be pooled in the federation and the sovereignty retained by the national states. The powers of a federated U.N. would be specifically confined to common needs and common dangers.

So far as jurisdiction over the individual is concerned, it would be restricted to those matters affecting the security of all peoples. The Nuremberg trials, it will be recalled, proceeded on the principle of individual responsibility and guilt for acts leading to war. What is needed now is exactly the same principle, except that this time the guilty parties should be apprehended in time to avert war rather than after the damage has been done and the dead counted.

Economic development, especially in the case of Asia and Africa, should be a signal opportunity for the federated U.N. It should be recognized, however, that many of the nations of Asia and Africa are just extricating themselves from a century or more of outside rule and that nothing should be done which could be regarded by those states as interference with their problems of internal development and control. Hence, it should be made clear that any requests for economic, technological, or scientific assistance to individual nations are to originate from the nations themselves. The greatest care should be taken to see that each development project would operate in a way consistent with each nation's own culture and institutions and that its own facilities and human resources would be fully utilized.

The U.N. already has within it many excellent agencies – in the fields of world health, food, refugee problems, education, science, and so forth. But two things are in the way of their effective operation. The first is that these groups lack any real authority or the means of carrying out the necessary programmes. The second is that the dominant energies and resources of most of the nations are being diverted to military purposes. The combination of authority and means could enable the special agencies of the U.N. to demonstrate high usefulness in improving the conditions of human existence.

Those agencies, of course, would be directly responsible to, and established by, the legislative branch of the U.N.

Where would all this authority be lodged? In the General Assembly? The Security Council? It is doubtful that the big states would like to see important powers given to the General Assembly in its present form, in view of the fact that they are on an even footing with states with only a fraction of their own populations. Meanwhile, the Security Council, run by the big states, is bound by the unanimity principle. This means that no issue of consequence involving the major nations can be settled at present on the basis of strict adherence to law, for a major nation could negate the law through the veto.

Any attempt to redefine the authority of the General Assembly and Security Council, however, squarely opens up the entire question both of representation and of division of powers.

If a purely democratic basis were used for representation, then two or three populous nations might be able to dominate the voting. As pointed out earlier, if a one-vote-for-one-state system obtained, a few small states with perhaps an aggregate population of twenty million might be able to outvote nations with an aggregate population of seven hundred and fifty million or more. This is perhaps the thorniest problem of all. There can be no authority without representation, but representation under existing circumstances seems impossible.

This dilemma may yield to the concept of dual federalism based on a regional approach inside the United Nations. Under this arrangement the General Assembly could be divided into its component regional parts, each of which would receive a total of one hundred votes or less, depending upon population, size, resources, and other vital factors. Each region would determine for itself the voting procedures for its own members in arriving at decisions concerning the vote that would be cast by the unit as a whole. A regional unit consisting of, say, ten members, two of which had a combined population larger than the combined total of the remaining eight members, might wish to give proportionate weight to the larger members in working out an equitable system of representation within itself on any question.

The advantage of the regional arrangement goes far beyond the possible solution it offers to the impasse of representation by population as against representation by nation. It recognizes a certain grouping of interests on the regional level – economic, cultural, political – and provides the means by which these natural interests could be protected and advanced.

The only questions on which the regional units need be called upon to vote as units in the General Assembly would be on matters involving the common security, or on relations of units to each other, or on the relations of members of one unit to members of another.

Dual federalism, then, is federalism of nations within regional units, and federalism of nations as members of regional units on the world level. The nation, the regional unit, and the federated U.N. would each exercise such sovereignty as was natural to it. The individual nations would have authority and jurisdiction in all matters pertaining to their own institutions and internal affairs. The regional units would have authority and jurisdiction in all matters pertaining to the regional needs and interests of its members. Finally, a federated U.N. would have authority and jurisdiction in those matters directly affecting the safety and vital needs of the world community.

As part of this general proposal, the Security Council might have to be reconstituted as an Executive Council. Its primary function would be to carry out the wishes and enforce the decisions of the General Assembly. All the special agencies – disarmament, atomic controls, world health, food, economic development, refugees, and so forth – of the U.N. would come within the administration of the Council.

The operating budget of the Council and its agencies would have to come before the General Assembly, which would have powers of appropriation and review.

The Executive Council, unlike its predecessor, the Security Council, would not be concerned with votes or vetoes within itself. It would not be a legislative agency but the principal enforcement arm of the United Nations. As such, it could make recommendations, but it could not enact legislation or review it.

Judicial review of legislation enacted by the General Assembly, and of the enforcement activities of the Executive Council, would be vested in a World Court.

So far we have been discussing the structured form of a world under law as an alternative to anarchy and nuclear force. Ultimately, however, the *form* of the peace is not enough. It is to be hoped that eventually an *ideology* of the peace will emerge – one that will enable increasingly large numbers of people to develop new and exciting concepts of loyalty to the human community. For all men – whether they go by the name of Americans or Russians or Chinese or British or Malayans or Indians or Africans – have obligations to one another that transcend their obligations to their sovereign societies.

The conflicts that involve twentieth-century man are not solely ideological or political. They are personal, historic, transcendent. They involve his relationship to others all the way from the immediate community that surrounds him to the human commonwealth as a whole.

These conflicts can be resolved in terms of first principles:

If there is a conflict between the security of the sovereign state and the security of the human commonwealth, the human commonwealth comes first.

If there is a conflict between the well-being of the nation

and the well-being of mankind, the well-being of mankind comes first.

If there is a conflict between the needs of this generation and the needs of all the later generations, the needs of the later generations come first.

If there is a conflict between the rights of the state and the rights of man, the rights of man come first. The state justifies its existence only as it serves and safeguards the rights of man.

If there is a conflict between public edict and private conscience, private conscience comes first.

If there is a conflict between the easy drift of prosperity and the ordeal of peace, the ordeal of peace comes first.

With these first principles in operation, the people can create a mandate for government. Such a mandate would enable the nation to put first things first. The nation can declare that, even in its self-defence, it will not engage in a war that would destroy the rest of the world. Neither will it hesitate to declare that it would rather die than be the first to use chemical, biological, or nuclear weapons on human beings.

It could declare that it considers it a privilege to commit and dedicate everything it has – its resources, energy, knowledge, and moral imagination – to the making of a genuine peace under justice and law.

All things are possible if we do not crave the distinction of being the last generation of men on earth.

DANILO DOLCI

Danilo Dolci, who was born in 1924, trained as an architect at the Faculty of Architecture, Milan Polytechnic, and the Conservatory, Rome. He later became a social worker and writer. He was the joint founder of the Christian Community at Nomadelfia. In 1958 he opened five centres for the unemployed in Sicily and in the same year won the Lenin Peace Prize.

This essay is in the form of a letter to a friend.

SOME time ago you asked me to write a few pages for you on 'ethical disobedience as a moral imperative in certain circumstances'. I must confess on opening your letter, I felt called upon to do something which, in a sense, was completely unnecessary. To quibble over a matter which to me seems already self-evident; so much part of myself, that I feel my time only properly used when devoted to *behaving* in this way and *living* in this way.

And yet your letter says: 'You are wrong, I tell you ... do what you deem to be right, do not listen to other people ... millions have gone to wage wars, morality does not enter into it. For a better life, they told us, and we believed what they said, just as much as you do now in what is virtually your own war, and in which the defeated will only be you yourself and your own children. Your struggle is great – but the idea of destroying oneself for the purpose of creating is absurd ... ' And I do not seek merely to be polite to you, allowing the argument to drop just because I love and respect you as a friend, nor in order to justify my decisions.

I am writing to you in the interim between one trend of ideas and another, noting down observations hurriedly, and sending a copy of these thoughts to friends who have asked for them.

1. Why is it that the verb 'obey' has come to be, in various parts of the world, not only a disagreeable but also a negative term? Perhaps because we are able to 'obey' in an external sense while simultaneously 'disobeying' within ourselves. How infinitely preferable we should find it if a man's obedience stemmed from a conscious act of his will.

2. It is urgent that men listen to one another; not shut themselves up in the limitations of their own opinion. Yet it is equally essential to analyse facts objectively within one's

A MATTER OF LIFE

own consciousness, being as open as possible about the process.

Joining a group is an efficient way of overcoming personal inadequacies by a process of integration and absorption within the whole; moreover, an effective communion may have compensating results. But being able to achieve less than one has set out to achieve, does not mean one's humanity is diminished in any way. The proper functioning and vitality of a group – the community itself – relies on the ability of each member to stand firmly by his own enlightened ideas, and entrusting the ultimate analysis to the deepest sense of values of each one. It follows then that, as a member of a group and at the same time a conscientious objector, every action is in itself carried out with a living conviction, and not merely an outward display of obedience or disobedience.

3. Of course, in the context of the relationship between an individual and a group, it is important to know how to distinguish clearly between the endless complex differences; between the humility which, unless it be true, may result in an acceptance of something which is important only for itself alone – fanatical enthusiasm, lack of discernment; the danger of submitting 'lovingly' at the expense of a loss of clarity and a sense of urgency; the danger of placing loyalty to the group higher than loyalty to truth, or to one's fellows, and so on.

To simplify this: obedience and disobedience as such have no meaning in themselves; it is unimportant whether one agrees or disagrees with official policies – what counts is doing what is true and right.

4. It becomes ever easier (in a world daily becoming more and more complex, of ever-increasing dimensions, ever more and more deluded by the tools of propaganda) to feel oneself fraught with personal insufficiencies, drifting on towards a mistaken humility, resigning oneself to thinking and living at second-hand. It struck me, particularly in New York and

DANILO DOLCI

those immense industrial undertakings of the U.S.S.R. the more vast and inhuman they become, the more awareness and curiosity are blunted; one becomes robo (and what a lot of human beings in those zones of recent Soviet industrialization are drunk with mass production), incapable of asking oneself the most elementary questions. How much more urgent it is then to rediscover fundamentals; namely, what is true and vital to life and to humane standards. On these alone is it possible to rebuild more firmly and surely.

It is on these values that our Centre for the Development of Western Sicily is founded; on self-scrutiny and on the efforts from below towards organized planning. Just now, among other things, we have written: 'One quality above all do we prize in our work, the quality of being connected with our convictions and our life, or the life we envisage in the future. When our enterprise becomes more culturally organized, then relationships will be based on common ground; all will feel themselves simultaneously members of the group and yet at the heart of an individual consciousness – conscientious objectors in that sense.'

In practice this means:

(*a*) constant recognition of initiative and the maintaining of the thread of a cultural ideal we feel to be our own;

(*b*) determination to identify what is important and absorb this into our initiative, and improve on those technical instruments indispensable to development, so that with these improvements there shall be no interference with the progress of our work;

(*c*) gauging the extent of assimilation – or of expansion – faithfully, but using the yardstick of presence of mind and wisdom of maturity;

(*d*) getting in contact with, and exchanging requirements with those peoples throughout the world who are investigating the latest methods, so that we shall feel ourselves similar to them.

There is then a need for each of us to seek deeper and make new discoveries and to align ourselves with what we have chosen to do.

5. Emphasizing the value of belonging to a group, it should be pointed out that those societies who are unified only on a territorial basis are not really unified, except as a temporary measure for some special purpose. The more the fundamental principles of a group, or an individual, differ from those of society, the more conflicts will exist, indeed must exist. These conflicts must, of course, be dealt with legitimately (and the choice of ways of dealing with them is important) and *actively*. I italicize the word because it may be insufficient to remain passive and 'disobey' in the sense of doing nothing; this in itself is too simple and from the beginning is seen to be insufficient. But in order to win, a different stand must be taken up – to be, or try to be, more active and capable of creating an advantageous substitute for the attitude which has been criticized. It is essential that the struggle must in itself possess the attributes of a new development resting on firmer and surer disciplines; seeds of a new and better organization.

6. 'My dear friend,' you write, 'ethics do not come into it.' I see what you mean, yet to me it seems that herein lies the key to the whole situation. Among the masses, especially in countries where research into ethics has never been encouraged, careful scrutiny and open discussion has not been encouraged either. Thus it is not realized generally that human behaviour has progressed from time immemorial and continues to progress. It is not understood, for example, that the ancient law of Moses, 'an eye for an eye and a tooth for a tooth', was in fact a great advance on previous laws which were based on force and force alone. At that time,

when force had the upper hand, it was considered to be the only true authority. Ethics have changed the situation and will continue to do so. It is not generally realized that it is through ethics alone that humanitarian standards will finally be achieved, obtaining their sustenance from the consciousness of each one of us.

7. Another important link, as I see it, is to bear in mind how much more advanced are ideal human standards than those of the legislature, incorporating as they do the remains of more primitive codes of behaviour. It is here that gaps, contradictions and basic conflicts abound between humanitarian ethics and official ethics, with all their old and dangerous encrustations.

If one believes that an individual who practises ethical disobedience is merely manifesting a spirit of personal revolt, then it may well be the fault of the individual himself that he gives the impression of being more of a rebel than a true revolutionary. I would repeat that we are face to face with an urgent need for an 'inner life', for a stricter discipline which aims at increasingly uniting us as human beings. Yet at the same time willing to co-operate wherever possible with the various strata of officialdom and careful to avoid corruption.

8. It is sufficient to look about one – and you must forgive me if I begin with myself when trying to clarify a few fundamental issues. For instance, using conscience as my mentor, how could I, as an architect, agree to build barracks and brothels instead of schools and hospitals? Could I allow myself to build houses intended only for the rich and those who need them least of all?

Ten years ago in Sicily I chose my way, and if the urban authorities had shown a little feeling after the excavation and work of a social-economic nature had been carried out (if I had not wished to consolidate in stone or even in an aesthetic sense the injustices and irrationalities of that

A MATTER OF LIFE

moment), could I have agreed to the request of their representative, pistol in hand, to clear out?

Could I have agreed that children be allowed to die because they were not fed or attended to, even though there was no actual law in force that considered it a crime to let a child die?

Could I have submitted to the continued ill-treatment of men and women in Western Sicily who were fired at by order of the government, instead of given an opportunity to work and educate themselves?

Could we have listened to, for instance, official orders to cease work on broken roads formerly impassable, while we had time to spare and were willing to be useful to ourselves and others?

Can we now allow life to continue being chaotically wasted while we await the convenience of the powers-that-be (even the Mafia recognizes its own laws), while a policy of non-violent, educational planning for the organized development of the area could be carried out, producing real benefits for all?

To put it briefly – when the best elements of mankind have agreed, after a thousand years of experience, which road it is preferable for human beings to tread, what right have we to deny it? The superiority of that road over all the others in its scholastic, cultural and religious aspects has been pointed out to us, notwithstanding the thousands of absurd contradictions that occur from time to time. Can we accept the fact that our state, our world, should use our talents, our lives, as instruments of destruction, instead of to feed, cure, enlighten and develop? What kind of men should we be if we accepted this? What kind of life should we be prepared to resign ourselves to in the future?

All this seems to me so absolutely obvious (even though few may not realize it yet) that it is futile to continue with self-analysis with its rhetorical risks, especially after the horrible light of the atom bomb has thrown up the argument in brilliant relief. Still, I will enclose the pages I wrote on the subject, on another occasion (the reports at the Peace Congresses in Moscow and New Delhi).

But there is one other thing I should like to emphasize: It is often through the efforts of those 'rebels' that I mentioned earlier on that improvements and advancements in legislation are obtained. For instance, look at the urgent struggle experienced in Italy for the promotion of a Republican Constitution.

9. You write: 'The idea of destroying oneself in order to create is absurd ... ' I realize that here you refer to a particular undertaking of mine – that of fasting.

Of course I do agree with you that to create one must also create within oneself as well. It is a reciprocal and interdependent thing. But you must concur with me in thinking that this aspect of life is still highly complex, I might even say mysterious. Sometimes a physical sacrifice of one's health and strength is the only thing that will cause events to thrust forward. It is a tragic fact, and I might well agree, *that in this there is something of absurdity*, but I know you realize what I mean.

Public fasting – or any other comparable act (not to be approached formalistically, as something positive in itself) – is a means one is obliged to use at certain times when a grave problem must be solved and all other methods fail. It is a means by which it is possible to:

(*a*) descend to a different state of being, becoming as one with all those who suffer the most;

(*b*) communicate more directly with the consciousness of others (or communicate with their conscience in the sense of knowledge plus ethical intelligence) who, as a rule, are subject to distractions rendering them unaware of the problem you face, rather than deliberately cruel;

(*c*) confirm one's faith in mankind; who will not

willingly allow one of themselves to die knowingly in an effort to save themselves;

(*d*) summon up a sense of responsibility in all, and more especially in those with the greatest responsibility.

10. And now I must stop, if I want to get this posted and away. I do not know if what I have noted down here will tell you anything direct, or how much of it will be of any use to you. Write to me, I shall endeavour to understand what you have to say. Perhaps one day we shall even be able to meet and find a comprehension based on a deeper reciprocal understanding that will help us to collaborate on those many aspects which we may well have in common.

With affection and gratitude,
Yours,
DANILO

ERICH FROMM

Dr Erich Fromm was born in Frankfurt in 1900, and studied psychology, sociology and philosophy at Frankfurt, Heidelberg, and Munich Universities. He graduated from the Berlin Institute of Psychoanalysis in 1931. Since 1955, he has been Head of the Department of Psychoanalysis of the Medical School of the National University of Mexico, and is Professor of Psychology at New York University.

For centuries kings, priests, feudal lords, industrial bosses and parents have insisted that *obedience is a virtue and that disobedience is a vice*. In order to introduce another point of view, let us set against this position the following statement: *human history began with an act of disobedience, and it is not unlikely that it will be terminated by an act of obedience.*

Human history was ushered in by an act of disobedience according to the Hebrew and Greek myths. Adam and Eve, living in the Garden of Eden, were part of nature; they were in harmony with it, yet did not transcend it. They were in nature as the foetus is in the womb of the mother. They were human, and at the same time not yet human. All this changed when they disobeyed an order. By breaking the ties with earth and mother, by cutting the umbilical cord, man emerged from a pre-human harmony, and was able to take the first step into independence and freedom. The act of disobedience set Adam and Eve free and opened their eyes. They recognized each other as strangers, and the world outside them as strange and even hostile. Their act of disobedience broke the primary bond with nature and made them individuals. 'Original sin', far from corrupting man, set him free; it was the beginning of history; man had to leave the Garden of Eden in order to learn to rely on his own powers and to become fully human.

The prophets, in their Messianic concept, confirmed the idea that man had been right in disobeying; that he had not been corrupted by his 'sin', but freed from the fetters of pre-human harmony. For the prophets, *history* is the place where man becomes human; during its unfolding he develops his powers of reason and of love until he creates a new harmony between himself, his fellow man and nature. This new harmony is described as 'the end of days', that period of history in which there is peace between man and

A MATTER OF LIFE

man, and between man and nature. It is a 'new' paradise created by man himself, and one which he only could create because he was forced to leave the 'old' paradise as a result of his disobedience.

Just as the Hebrew myth of Adam and Eve so the Greek myth of Prometheus sees all of human civilization based on an act of disobedience. Prometheus, in stealing the fire from the gods, lays the foundation for the evolution of man. There would be no human history were it not for Prometheus's 'crime'. He, like Adam and Eve, is punished for his disobedience. But he does not repent and ask for forgiveness. On the contrary, he proudly says: 'I would rather be chained to this rock than be the obedient servant of the gods.'

Man has continued to evolve by acts of disobedience. Not only that, his spiritual development was possible only because there were men who dared to say no to the powers-that-be in the name of their conscience or their faith, but also his intellectual development was dependent on the capacity for being disobedient. Disobedient to authorities who tried to muzzle new thoughts and to the authority of long-established opinions which declared a change to be nonsense.

If the capacity for disobedience constituted the beginning of human history, obedience might very well cause the end of human history. I am not speaking symbolically or poetically. There is the possibility, or even the probability, that the human race will destroy civilization and even all life upon earth within the next five to ten years. There is no rationality or sense in it. But the fact is that while we are living technically in the Atomic Age the majority of men – including most of those who are in power – live emotionally still in the Stone Age. That while our mathematics, astronomy and the natural sciences are of the twentieth century, most of our ideas about politics, the state and society lag far behind the age of science. If mankind commits suicide it will be because people will obey those who command them to push the deadly buttons; because they will obey the archaic passions of fear, hate and greed, because they will obey obsolete clichés of state sovereignty and national honour. The Soviet leaders talk much about revolutions, and we in the 'free world' talk much about freedom. Yet they and we discourage disobedience – in the Soviet Union explicitly and by force – in the free world implicitly and by the more subtle methods of persuasion.

By all this I do not mean to say that all disobedience is a virtue and all obedience a vice. Such a view would ignore the dialectical relationship between obedience and disobedience. Whenever the principles which are obeyed and those which are disobeyed are irreconcilable, an act of obedience to one principle is necessarily an act of disobedience to its *counterpart*, and vice versa. Antigone is the classic example of this dichotomy. By obeying the inhuman laws of the state Antigone necessarily would disobey the laws of humanity. By obeying the latter, she must disobey the former. All martyrs of religious faiths, of freedom, and of science have had to disobey those who wanted to muzzle them, in order to obey their own consciences, the laws of humanity and of reason. If a man can only obey and not disobey, he is a slave; if he can only disobey and not obey, he is a rebel – not a revolutionary; he acts out of anger, disappointment, resentment, yet not in the name of a conviction or a principle.

However, in order to prevent a confusion of terms an important qualification must be made. Obedience to a person, institution or power (heteronomous obedience) is submission; it implies the abdication of my autonomy and the acceptance of a foreign will or judgment in place of my own. Obedience to my own reason or conviction (autonomous obedience) is not an act of submission but one of affirmation. My conviction and my judgment, if authentically mine, are part of me. If I follow them rather than the judgment of others, I am being myself; hence the word 'obey' can be applied only in a metaphorical sense and with a meaning which is fundamentally different from the one in the case of 'heteronomous obedience'.

But this distinction needs still two further qualifications; one with regard to the concept of conscience, and the other with regard to the concept of authority.

The word 'conscience' is used to express two phenomena which are quite distinct from each other. One is the 'authoritarian conscience' which is the internalized voice of an authority whom we are eager to please and afraid of displeasing. This authoritarian conscience is what most people experience when they obey their conscience. It is also the conscience which Freud speaks of, and which he called 'Super-Ego'. This Super-Ego represents the internalized commands and prohibitions of father, accepted by the son out of fear. Different from the authoritarian conscience is the 'humanistic conscience'; this is the voice present in every human being and independent from external sanctions and rewards. Humanistic conscience is based on the fact that as human beings we have an intuitive knowledge of what is human and inhuman, what is conducive of, and what is destructive of life. This conscience serves our functioning as human beings. It is the voice which calls us back to ourselves, to our humanity.

Authoritarian conscience (Super-Ego) is still obedience to a power outside of myself, even though this power has been internalized. Consciously I believe that I am following *my* conscience; in effect, however, I have swallowed the principles of *power*; just because of the illusion that humanistic conscience and Super-Ego are identical, internalized authority is so much more effective than the authority which is clearly experienced as not being part of me. Obedience to the 'authoritarian conscience', like all obedience to outside thoughts and power, tends to debilitate 'humanistic conscience', the ability to be and to judge oneself.

The statement, on the other hand, that obedience to another person is *ipso facto* submission needs also to be qualified by distinguishing 'irrational' from 'rational' authority. An example of 'rational authority' is to be found in the relation between student and teacher; one of 'irrational

authority' in the relationship between slave and m
Both relationships are based on the fact that the autho1
the person in command is accepted. Dynamically, hov
they are of a different nature. The interests of the teacher
and the student (in the ideal case) lie in the same direction.
The teacher is satisfied if he succeeds in furthering the
student; if he has failed to do so, the failure is his and the
student's. The slave owner, on the other hand, wants to
exploit the slave as much as possible. The more he gets out
of him the more satisfied he is. At the same time, the slave
tries to defend as best he can his claims for a minimum of
happiness. The interests of slave and master are antagonistic,
because what is advantageous to the one is detrimental to
the other. The superiority of the one over the other has a
different function in each case; in the first it is the condition
for the furtherance of the person subjected to the authority;
in the second, it is the condition for his exploitation. Another
distinction runs parallel to this: 'rational authority' is
rational because the authority, whether it is held by a
teacher or a captain of a ship giving orders in an emergency,
acts in the name of reason which, being universal, I can
accept without submitting. Irrational authority has to use
force or suggestion, because no one would let himself be
exploited if he were free to prevent it.

Why is man so prone to obey and why is it so difficult for
him to disobey? As long as I am obedient to the power of
the state, the Church, public opinion, I feel safe and protected. In fact it makes little difference what power it is that
I am obedient to. It is always an institution, or men, who use
force in one form or another – and who fraudulently claim
omniscience and omnipotence. My obedience makes me part
of the power I worship, and hence I feel strong. I can make
no error, since it decides for me; I cannot be alone because it
watches over me; I cannot commit a sin because it does not
let me do so, and even if I do sin, the punishment is only the
way of returning to the almighty power.

A MATTER OF LIFE

In order to disobey, one must have the courage to be alone, to err, and to sin. But courage is not enough. The capacity for courage depends on a person's state of development. Only if a person has emerged from mother's lap and father's commands, only if he has emerged as a fully developed individual and thus has acquired the capacity to think and feel for himself, only then can he have the courage to say no to power, to disobey.

A person can become free through acts of disobedience by learning to say no to power; but the capacity for disobedience is not only the condition for freedom; freedom is also the condition for disobedience. If I am afraid of freedom, I cannot dare to say no, I cannot have the courage to be disobedient. Indeed, freedom and the capacity for disobedience are inseparable; hence any social, political, and religious system which proclaims freedom yet stamps out disobedience, cannot speak the truth.

There is another reason why it is so difficult to dare to disobey, to say no to power. During most of human history obedience has been identified with virtue – disobedience with sin. The reason is simple: thus far during most of history a minority has ruled over the majority. This rule was made necessary by the fact that there was only enough of the good things of life for the few, and only the crumbs remained for the many. If the few wanted to enjoy the good things and, beyond that, to have the many serve them and work for them, one condition was necessary: the many had to learn obedience. To be sure, obedience can be established by sheer force. But this method has many disadvantages. It constitutes a constant threat that one day the many might have the means to overthrow the few by force; furthermore there are many kinds of work which cannot be done properly if nothing but fear is behind the obedience. Hence the obedience which is only rooted in the fear of force must be transformed into one rooted in man's heart. Man must want, and even need, to obey, instead of only fearing to disobey. If this is to be achieved, power must assume the qualities of the All Good, of the All Wise, it must become All Knowing. If this happens, power can proclaim that disobedience is sin, and obedience virtue, and once this has been proclaimed, the many can accept obedience because it is good, and detest disobedience because it is bad, rather than to detest themselves for being cowards. Then indeed the principle is established which Luther once put in these words: 'Therefore let us everyone who can, smite, slay and stab, secretly or openly, remembering that *nothing can be more poisonous, hurtful or devilish than a rebel.*' From Luther to the nineteenth century one was concerned with overt and explicit authorities. Luther, the Pope, the princes, wanted to uphold it; the middle class, the workers, the philosophers, tried to uproot it. The fight against authority in the state as well as in the family was often the very basis for the development of an independent and daring person. The fight against authority was inseparable from the intellectual mood which characterized the philosophers of the enlightenment, and the scientists. This 'critical mood' was one of faith in reason, and at the same time of doubt in everything which is said or thought, in as much as it is based on tradition, superstition, custom, power. The principles *sapere aude* and *de omnibus es dubitandum*, 'dare to be wise' and 'of all one must doubt' were characteristic of the attitude which permitted and furthered the capacity to say no.

Where is authority today? In the totalitarian countries it is overt authority of the state, supported by the strengthening of respect for authority in the family and in the school. The Western democracies, on the other hand, feel proud at having overcome nineteenth-century authoritarianism. But have they – or has only the character of the authority changed?

This century is the century of the hierarchically organized bureaucracies in government, business, and labour unions. These bureaucracies administer things *and* men as one;

they follow certain principles, especially the economic principle of the balance sheet, quantification, maximal efficiency, and profit, and they function essentially as an electronic computer would that has been programmed with these principles. The individual becomes a number, transforms himself into a thing. But just because there is no overt authority, because he is not 'forced' to obey, the individual is under the illusion that he acts voluntarily, that he is following only his own will and decision, or that he follows only 'rational' authority. Who can disobey the 'reasonable', who can disobey the computer-bureaucracy, who can disobey when he is not even aware of obeying? In the family and in education the same thing happens. The corruption of the theories of progressive education has led to a method where the child is not told what to do, not given orders, nor punished for failure to execute them. The child just 'expresses himself'. But he is filled from the first day of his life onward with an unholy respect for conformity, with the fear of being 'different', with the fright of being away from the rest of the herd. The 'organization man' thus reared in the family and in the school, and having his education completed in the big organization, has opinions but no convictions; he amuses himself, but is unhappy; he is even willing to sacrifice his life and that of his children in voluntary obedience to the impersonal and anonymous powers. He accepts the calculation of deaths which has become so fashionable in the discussions on thermonuclear war: half the population of a country dead – 'quite acceptable'; two-thirds dead – 'maybe not'.

The case of Eichmann is symbolic of our situation and has a significance far beyond the one which his accusers in the courtroom in Jerusalem were concerned with. Eichmann is a symbol of the organization man, of the alienated bureaucrat for whom men, women and children have become numbers. He is a symbol of all of us. We can see ourselves in Eichmann – but the most frightening thing about him is that after the entire story is told in terms of his own admissions, he is able in perfect good faith to plead his innocence. It is clear that if he were once more in the same situation he would do it again. And so would we – and so do we.

The organization man has lost the capacity to disobey, he is not even aware of the fact that he obeys. At this point in history the capacity to doubt, to criticize, and to disobey, may be all that stands between a future for mankind and the end of civilization.

SHINZO HAMAI

Shinzo Hamai was born in Japan in 1905. He graduated from the Law Department of Tokyo University in 1931 and has been Mayor of Hiroshima since 1947.

LOOKING back from the present day, when giant megatons are blasted away in nuclear experiments, the atomic bomb that was exploded over Hiroshima on August 6, 1945, was indeed a mere 'baby'. None the less, the lesson it brought home to us was a far-reaching one. To the minds of those of the Hiroshima citizens who saw with their own eyes what a catastrophe the tiny bomb brought with it to the city and people of Hiroshima, it occurred almost intuitively that nothing less than a total annihilation of mankind would be the outcome of the ever-advancing science and productivity, should these be made to serve destructive purposes. That this was not a groundless apprehension seems to have been borne out by the past seventeen years that have intervened.

At the time when nuclear weapons, six to ten thousand times more powerful than the one used on Hiroshima, are in production – with every prospect of still larger types to come in the not so distant future – it may be worth while to remember that a single nuclear bomb blasted away all the houses of Hiroshima and that an estimated two hundred thousand or more were killed indiscriminately, regardless of age or sex. Even now, the radiation effects lingering in the bodies of the exposed survivors threaten them with the sudden incidence of various sicknesses, that frequently lead to premature death – a fact of primary importance that should receive serious consideration.

War used to be a last resort when the existence of a nation was at stake. But a nuclear war, it should now be clearly borne in mind, would no longer serve such a purpose, for the primary aim of self-defence would be defeated in a world-wide devastation which would not only make the word 'victory' meaningless, but might even entail complete extermination of mankind.

A MATTER OF LIFE

It is high time that all people of the world stood up and tried once again to arouse the conscience of those peoples and nations which, being well aware of the wartime international law condemning even the bacteriological and poison-gas warfare as inhumane, still presume upon the use of nuclear weapons. At the same time, all nations and peoples should abandon self-seeking adherence to their own selfish claims and demands and instead, at this time, when it is still not too late, exert honest efforts towards the banning of nuclear weapons and complete elimination of wars. There is no more sense in tampering with ideological controversies than in scrambling for things on board when the ship is about to sink.

EYO ITA

Dr Eyo Ita was born in 1903 at Creek Town, Calabar, Nigeria. He attended Columbia and London Universities. He initiated the National Education Movement in 1936 and is at present the Principal and Proprietor of the West African Peoples' Institute, which he founded in 1938. He has been a leader in his country's struggle for independence.

THE steady drift to atomic doom on which the human race is going demands that we should pause and think. No one can doubt the fact that men and women in all lands are today longing 'with longing as intense as pain' for peace and goodwill, sole condition of progress and happiness on earth. The strangest paradox of all is that while we desire peace so intensely we are moving steadily and unmistakably towards war in which nuclear weapons are sure to be used. A friend of mine has called the situation 'madness', nuclear madness! Of course it is madness, stark insanity! Men desiring one thing ardently, and yet doing that which produces the exact opposite of what they desire!

'In spite of "Fears", Pride rules our Wills'

It is grim and sad that with all the amazing resources of twentieth-century mankind – with all the intellectual and cultural achievements, with the effective conquest of nature and exploitation of the material resources which give man so much power that he can boast of 'having dominion over all things', he is today pitifully helpless in the face of the situation which he himself has created with his own hands. An observer viewing the human race from some distant planet might wonder with pity why a creature so well endowed with greatness and power should be so futile, so infantile, so ineffective in coping with the very situation which he himself has created. The fact is that we are insane, unable to 'think'. Humanity is not one. We are not integrated. That part of us that desires peace is different from, and at war with, the other part that wants war. This inherent civil war is one root of our futility and frustration.

It would seem as if the proud men of power in each national group want one thing while the masses of the people want another; that strong nations or blocks of them seek political prestige and economic power and position, while the masses want friendship and goodwill and harmony.

But the situation is not quite so simple. We are not simple fools. Our stupidity is compounded with sin. The pride which motivates the arrogant national leaders and world mighty ones is deep in the flesh and blood of the masses, blinding all of us, and tempting all to move towards the very things we most dread. So, 'in spite of "fears", pride rules our wills.' The politician does everything he can to maintain the prestige and pride of his nation because his people desire that prestige must be maintained, and arrogance matched with arrogance. The governments are basically what the people are, and in them are intensified the basic selfishness and infantile pride and stupidity of the individuals. As Reinhold Niebuhr insists, the individual may in his sober private moments rise to lofty moral spiritual heights, but the society, that is man-in-the-group, is spiritually imbecile. The moral tide of man-in-the-group is ever so low.

Moreover modern society itself becomes so vast, so complex and so impersonal that the spiritual initiative of the individual is atrophied. But must this be? Where then is man's claim to freedom and to dignity?

The temptation to infantile show of power and pride is ever with us, strongest in the strongest, and weakest in the weakest, but none is immune. People are not tempted in what they do not possess.

Such is the plight of the rival possessors of the nuclear weapons. But such too is the plight of us all. We are all engulfed in one swirling fate. We must wake to the truth. We must come to a realization of our plight. We must be wide awake to the peril we are heading towards.

There are not a few who believe that another catastrophic world war will never come because men know enough of the peril involved, and that there is enough deterrence in the amount of fear felt by all, and in the common knowledge that the atomic weapon is no longer the monopoly of any one man or nation.

The truth is that the human race is yet very infantile. In the middle of the twentieth century this immature homo sapiens is fumbling in his swaddling clothes with powers in his hands far beyond his control. How many times has he not banged his little head against the 'Rock of Ages' even before the first half of this century is out? Who ever thought that the compatriots of Immanuel Kant, citizens of a country that could justly boast of being on the forefront of human progress, could rally in teeming millions round a madcap, only to be swept into colossal destruction such as man never heard of? Who can guess what would be our reactions if Nikita Krushchev or John Kennedy should lose his temper, and the first atomic bomb should explode on our wives and children? The youths who drove the tanks of 1940–1 had no memory of the disasters of 1917–18 and their causes. And it is now a much longer time since the disasters of 1939–45! What is there to prevent the same infantile reactions and the consequent tragedies?

'In spite of "Fears"'

Even assuming that we can remember all the horrors, and that we experience deep 'fears', fear of loss of lives and property, fear of destruction of all the monuments of culture, of fires and brimstone descending on all modern Sodoms and Gomorrahs, and fear of the extinction of all that we prize highest and love best, we know too well that no such negative emotion alone by itself can cure or tame the irresistible dynamic of pride and sinful stupidity. 'In spite of "fears", pride rules our wills.' We need a power more positive, more dynamic, a ruler of our 'wills' who is invincible, who can integrate all our wills and motives, and direct them to just and enduring peace.

We need a madness superior to nuclear madness to cure it

or 're-educate' it. Will the human race survive? Then there must be the 'will to survive', there must be a madness far superior to the 'nuclear madness', an insanity that can tame our sinful pride and infantile stupidity.

When I think of Bertrand Russell in his nineties in sheer defiance demonstrating against nuclear tests, I remember that superior insanity. I remember how Socrates with a similar madness became the instrument for the survival and triumph of reason and integrity at that hour in which reason and integrity were being threatened with annihilation. I remember the sublimest insanity, that of Gethsemane, when Absolute Truth-Love threatened with extinction won the survival and triumph of Absolute Truth-Love over hate and even death. When I so remember I take heart and despair leaves me. But this cannot be an easy victory.

Will the human race survive? 'If there is the will, then the thing itself is no longer a fable.' This was the reply that Herzl gave to a desperate race when confronted with the threat of extinction. If there is a genuine will to survive, then survival is no longer a fable.

Such a will is more than mere wishful thinking. More than ordinary determination, it is a fire, a passion, an insanity so powerful and so consuming that it always carries victory before it.

But where is the catalyst to help us to compose such a will, a visionary so dynamic, so clear-sighted that he or she has not only a full realization of the perils of modern atomic wars, but also a complete grasp and understanding of the beauty and glory of the destiny of man as a mature child of God? Who will come forward as a complete incarnation of man's humanity? Who will face the challenge of this moment, the call to create a ferment, to produce a *change* that will prevent annihilation and ensure survival of the human race? The will to survive must be composed, and I am sure God of Love can give us the faith passionate enough, the imagination so creative, so powerful, that we can achieve what now seems impossible.

EYO ITA

The Humanity of Man

Man's humanity is now being threatened with annihilation. Will it survive? We must not flippantly cherish easy hopes, for while the tender bud of humanity has successfully come 'o'er moor and fen, over crag and torrent', and, as an infant baby of a divine Parent who is Absolute Love, it has been well protected, as it were destined for a purpose, yet it has seen many a colossal tragedy, and may yet see more before it comes of age.

In our own generation we have seen it happen twice through sinful pride of powerful nation, through man's infantile stupidity, through 'vain imagination' of those who think themselves strong. These tragic experiences have been very costly. And we do not have to have them, for we are not, like the butterflies, helpless slaves of instincts. We are divine children, the inheritors of divine genes and chromosomes, born with the capacity to think and *to choose* between good and evil, and with plastic adaptability not given to other creatures. Man's humanity is an eternal heritage to be kept undefiled, to be put into maximum use.

One unmistakable aspect of man's humanity is *our capacity* to *change*, to think and choose, to act differently in response to strange circumstances in our environment, especially whenever such strange circumstances threaten our welfare and survival. As Sir Wilfrid Le Gros Clark told the British scientists at a recent conference at Norwich, England, man's humanity has biological foundations. Man's inventive capacity is based on his possession of a unique quality of brain. The Cortical Brain which is intimately interlocked with the Basal Brain and controlling it is the available neurological machinery whereby we can adapt ourselves to our changing environment. With this machinery our emotional and instinctive impulses can be subordinated to the good of the community as a whole.

Man's possession of the capacity to choose between right

and wrong, his possession of conscience, of what I have called his 'divine genes and chromosomes', along with his adaptability, has in the past enabled him to meet and triumph over threats of extinction. It has stood him in good stead before tragic circumstances that have destroyed the dinosaurs and other huge inadaptable monsters of the 'old world'. Throughout his relatively long period of emergence and development on earth this divine capacity has been of immeasurable service to man. Now by his own ingenuity man has created a *new environment* with new circumstances, a new geography and a new history. Faced with his new sociological and economic environment will his capacity to change and to choose be adequate? In the past he had used it successfully both as the individual and as 'man-in-the-group'.

Is there capacity to cope with man-created new environment: power politics, economic ambition and rivalry; absolute sovereignty of states; racial national pride; war culture and predatory mentality, nuclear armoury, cold war stimuli and space-age economy? Have we the capacity to think, to choose, and to change in the face of this *new* environment and its new circumstances? Have we the capacity for wider and loftier loyalties? Loyalty to the human race instead of loyalty to a petty, puny tribe? Respect for world law instead of infantile clinging to absolute sovereignty of states?

Sir Wilfrid points to increasing 'effective consciously directed co-operativeness' as the key to man's survival in the face of the present threat of annihilation. I agree. But have we the will? Assuming that we have the capacity, where is the will to survive? Where is the strategy, the *Means*, the *Way*?

Gandhi, insisting on the 'Right Means', offered the world 'Satyagraha', the Method of Absolute Truth-Love, a weapon which is invincible. Men and women must come forward who have so incarnated man's humanity in themselves that they become effective instruments for the survival of the humanity of man. They will constitute that *will*, that fire, that passion, that madness which is superior to the nuclear insanity. That madness must infect the surrounding human herd sufficiently to cause change.

Gandhi had insisted that those who desire 'change' must create ferments, must move the masses. There must be people who have so incarnated the cause in themselves that they cannot fail to consume the masses with the flame of their passion. I am sure God who is Absolute Truth-Love intends that humanity should survive. He will surely produce heroes and heroines of the hour, such heralds of the new human dawn, such buds of spring as will produce the necessary change that guarantees survival.

What we desperately need at this crisis is, not a bigger brain, not a more complex cortex, but a more sensitive conscience, a hero, a heroine with a consuming passion, a divine madness far superior to the nuclear insanity that now threatens our survival.

In the past our development had been mainly physical and biological – bigger and more complex brains, sharper and more discriminatory intellectual tools. Our creative inventive capacity was mainly applied to adapt man to the strange circumstances in his physical environment. But man is more than a physical entity. Man is a spirit. Man appears to reach his limits as a physical creature. The main area of his growth at present and in the future is spiritual. If he must cease to be infantile in his major responses in crises such as we are facing, then he must be spiritually more mature. As Mrs Eleanor Roosevelt has put it: 'The time has come when we must grow up.' Our conscience, our divine genes and chromosomes, must be better developed, more clearly discerning, more sensitive and responsive to moral and spiritual situations.

Already man has started creating strange circumstances and new environments that are more than physical. He is

A MATTER OF LIFE

creating not only new rockets and space-ships, not only artificial silks and synthetic rubber and glass; but new spiritual climates, new relationships of friendship and hostility, of fears and hopes, of conflict and co-operation, of harmony and incompatibility. Our brothers are no longer only our blood relations, but all who do our 'Father's will'. To attempt to meet 'new occasions' with old 'duties' is not only anachronistic but also disastrous. Man's basic spiritual genius, his plastic adaptability, must be applied effectively to meet the problems of the new spiritual environment which man himself has created. There must be the will adequately to do it.

It is quite obvious that the most vital problem facing our generation is how peace and friendship will be created among men and nations, how harmony will be achieved between one life and another, and within every life itself. The *summum bonum* of all achievements is the achievement of peace and goodwill among men and nations, of harmony in the life of every person.

As Gandhi insisted, we must apply the 'Right Means' to solve every problem, or never solve any at all. And the only Means, the only Way that works at all, is God's way. It is God's way that has served man in his successful response to his physical environment. In his new spiritual environment with its strange circumstances no other way will work. This way, as the Mahatma demonstrated it, is the Way of Truth and Absolute Love, the *via crucis*. In his great vision of God's grand piano, Kwegyir Aggrey saw it as spiritual harmony to be achieved through mutual service and respect. Sir Wilfrid's 'effective, consciously directed co-operativeness' is the scientific version of this key to survival. The will to survive must be composed of such fire, such passion, such divine stuff as constitute the strength and genius of a Gandhi, an Aggrey, and such other heralds of the new human dawn. To achieve anything with it is to accept it as God's will for man, as a 'categorical imperative' before which everything must yield.

EYO ITA

Cause must be Organized

Causes do not flourish by themselves and their unexploited merits. They must be incarnated in men and women, and they must be organized. The superior wisdom of the 'children of darkness' stems from the fact that they know how to organize evil. They make evil triumphant by organizing it. They strengthen their purpose by uniting their wills, by having one heart, one mind, a powerful integration of all their energies. They take hold of the available energies of matter and mind and organize them on a lower, more demonic level, as Harry Emerson Fosdick shows; and they achieve superior strength and success.

Why cannot the 'children of light' unite? Why can they not integrate their available energies and direct them to fulfil the purpose of God? The same energies of mind and matter are available to us all. The combative instinct, the capacity to herd together, to construct, to display, to will, to imagine. All the energies of matter – electric and atomic – are available for good causes, and the 'children of light' who have the will and the faith can integrate and direct them to achieve the purpose of God for man. Surely we can apply the creative, inventive capacity of man in our present crisis to such ends.

KENNETH KAUNDA

Kenneth Kaunda was born in 1924 at the Church of Scotland Mission near Chinsale in Northern Rhodesia, and was brought up amongst the Bemba people where he qualified as a teacher. In 1952 he was made Organizing Secretary of the A.N.C. and subsequently elected Secretary-General of the movement. Released from prison in 1960 after a long illness, he was elected President of the new United National Independent Party. Throughout his career he has held an unwavering belief in non-violence.

War with Communist China, according to Mr Nehru, is a possibility that India must face. Giving details to Parliament of recent Chinese incursions into Indian territory on the Himalayan frontier, the Prime Minister announced that India's strength was being brought up.
Observer, Sunday, May 6, 1962.

IN September 1961 I had the privilege and honour in New Delhi of being made the first Chairman of the Conference that was being held to discuss Portuguese colonialism in Africa. In my speech from the chair I took the opportunity to urge the Prime Minister of India, Pandit Nehru, to give a lead in defeating Portuguese colonialism by removing the Portuguese from Goa – even if this required the use of force. A few months later the Prime Minister of India invaded Goa and drove out the Portuguese by military means. I am not pretending that the Prime Minister of India acted because of my words; my purpose in reporting the speech I made is to identify myself with the action taken by the Indian Government.

The invasion of Goa met with a great amount of criticism from other countries, particularly those in the West. India, and those preachers of non-violence who supported her, were accused of being hypocritical, of preaching one philosophy and acting on another. Some people also find reports of the strength of the Indian army inconsistent with the philosophy of non-violence. It is suggested that India has now abandoned the teachings of Mahatma Gandhi, who taught India to put non-violence into practice.

It is true that, until the invasion of Goa, Pandit Nehru was universally accepted as a true follower of the Mahatma's teachings. From 1952 I also have personally professed to follow the Mahatma's method of non-violence; and I think that in trying to follow these methods my colleagues and I in Northern Rhodesia can rightly claim to have met with an astonishing amount of success. Why then did I call on the Prime Minister of India to remove the Portuguese even if it meant using force? Is this an admission of the impotence of methods of non-violence?

From time immemorial man has been using violence to settle disputes; 'might is right' has in practice largely been accepted. Countries have been conquered and reconquered; governments have been overcome and the new authorities themselves overthrown by violence, and the only concern of the vanquished was whether there was a possibility of gaining sufficient strength to renew the battle. Yet gradually there has spread the concept of settling disputes within a political unit by methods other than war. Constitutions providing for governments which are responsive to the desires of the people have removed the need for changes through violence, in certain territories, although the threat always remains, and the possibility of small and poor minorities, or even majorities, getting an effective say in their own government is often nullified in practice. Yet even now in large areas of the world governments maintain their power through the judicious use of force, or the threat of force, and there are peoples who are believed to acquiesce in the policies of their government simply because there seems no alternative – they do not feel that they could effectively overcome the force wielded by those in authority.

This was the situation in India when Gandhi gave form to non-violent principles as a means of expressing opposition and non-co-operation with the government. Gandhi was not the first man who preached and lived according to non-violent principles, but he was the first who, in a sense, codified these principles and advocated them as a means of mass action, as a means of the people's expression of their desires. It is since his time that non-violence or passive resistance has been used as a weapon to force governments to change their policies. As Gandhi expressed it: non-violence was a moral concept, but in the political field he regarded its practice as an experiment. To Gandhi this policy was right whether or not it was effective; to many of his followers, including myself, it is right, but it must also be effective – for we regard other things as also being matters of morality. We have used non-violent protest methods in Northern Rhodesia over a long period, first to deal with social injustices, and more recently for direct political purposes. As far back as 1946 the African Welfare Societies (which later came together to form the African National Congress) were passing resolution after resolution protesting against racial discrimination which was practised in public places, and asking the Northern Rhodesian Government to outlaw this by legislation.

There was plenty of need for this. Very many shops refused to serve their African customers inside, but insisted that Africans queue up outside at 'pigeon-holes' through which one, or at most two, assistants passed them the things they asked for. This meant that women carrying babies on their backs had to queue up in long lines exposed to the rain and cold in winter and the hot sun in summer. Butchers' shops in particular practised this discrimination and they further were in the habit of refusing to let Africans see what they were buying; if they tried to ask they were very rudely treated. This policy was followed by other shops, even those who allowed Africans to enter inside (Africans wishing to purchase a suit or a dress, or a sewing-machine, or any other similar item) would not permit them to examine the goods properly and obliged them to select their requirements just by looking at them from a distance. Furthermore, post offices and other government buildings practised the same sort of segregation. Special crowded sections for Africans and large, almost empty sections for Europeans – who could thus be served quickly and in comfort while Africans waited a long time just to buy a stamp or to get a form.

This situation continued because of the complete absence of political power among the African people of Northern

Rhodesia. While Europeans elected their representatives to the Legislative Council, the Africans had no voice at all; in theory the African interests were looked after by the civil servants in the government. It was even difficult for us to organize large-scale public meetings; these had to be conducted according to laid down procedures after permission had been obtained from the police. Very early in its life, too, the African National Congress discovered that many of its leaders were banned from speaking, or got themselves arrested, or were otherwise victimized for their activities.

Finally, in 1953, the A.N.C. decided that resolutions alone were not enough. We formed 'Action Groups' consisting of volunteers who were ready to perform any task assigned to them by the Congress. These volunteers went first to 'Training Centres' where we tried to give them an idea of the philosophy which we had learned by reading about the Indian struggle, and from Christ's teachings of turning the other cheek when your enemy hits you. We also instructed them in how to avoid violent clashes with the police and all those in authority. We warned them that they must not respond to provocation, and also of the consequences of the steps they were going to undertake, and of the beating-up and imprisonment which would almost certainly follow. I do not hesitate to say that the training given was not as good as we should have liked it to be and in some respects it was very poor. This was because none of us had had any opportunity to go deeply into the techniques of non-violent campaigns, and further, that the political difficulties which our organization was already experiencing meant that in many cases the only people available to run these training centres were people with less experience of, or understanding of, this approach.

When the time came for action, the members of the 'Action Groups' went out in tens, twenties, or even hundreds, to butchers' shops, department stores, post offices, and other places practising discrimination, which we had chosen as our targets; then they demanded normal civilized service. In almost every case the first reaction of the management was to call the police, and the second was to tell the 'Action Group' members to leave the premises. If they did not do so on the instant they were very often pushed and shoved by the police and on many occasions were really brutally beaten up and then arrested. During the five years these campaigns for social reforms continued, men, women and children were beaten up and imprisoned by the thousand. But this did not deter our people. On the contrary, despite the grave difficulties we had some notable successes. By 1957 pigeon-hole service had virtually disappeared from Lusaka, the capital, and had been greatly reduced in other areas. The segregation in post offices had been theoretically ended – although in practice this is still not completely true. Finally, in 1960, government passed legislation to outlaw racial discrimination in public places.

This new legislation is not completely satisfactory: it had no teeth in it. But in any case by that year the emphasis of the Nationalist struggle was no longer on social reforms, but on total political emancipation. This called for new techniques of resistance, but we still tried to operate non-violent methods.

The first time we felt the need to institute the new approach was only four and a half months after the Nationalist movement had passed through a crisis and split, with the majority forming the Zambia African National Congress. In March 1959 the Z.A.N.C. declared a boycott of what has become known as the Benson Constitution. The success of this boycott depended on getting support from the few Africans who were qualified to vote under this constitution – a few civil servants and a handful of Africans who had good jobs in commerce, industry, or mines. Thus our campaign, while being directed against the government on behalf of the mass of the people, had to get support from a small group of well-to-do African families whose self-interest required that they should support the government, or at least not come out openly in opposition to it. Despite evident difficulties of such an operation, it became obvious to the Governor that we were going to be successful. He then banned all public meetings, which meant the end of one of our most important forms of public demonstration.

On behalf of the Congress, I petitioned for the removal of this ban on meetings; in my third petition I gave notice that we should be compelled to ignore this ruling, regardless of the legal situation. When, therefore, we proceeded with our declared intention of calling 'illegal meetings' we knew what to expect – and of course we got it. On March 11, 1959, over one hundred of us were rounded up and sent into rustication in remote areas. Three months later, while still restricted in this way, I and a number of my colleagues were re-arrested and charged with 'conspiring to effect an unlawful purpose', and sentenced accordingly.

The second time we used non-violent passive resistance techniques to effect a political purpose was in July 1961, when H.M. Government in Britain declared its intention of imposing a new constitution which was again designed to keep the majority of the people in the political clutches of a privileged few. Our consultations with the Northern Rhodesian authorities and our delegations to Britain had brought no results. We were therefore left with no alternative but to take more direct action.

First we appealed to world leaders, asking them to use their good offices with the British Government. As this failed to yield any results we took the second step in our five-point master plan. This was for men to burn their identity certificates and for women to burn their marriage certificates – both of which were used for harassing purposes by the authorities.

We did this in five of our eight provinces and the government's reaction was immediate. Federal troops were called in when the Northern Rhodesian police failed to patrol the areas concerned adequately from their point of view. Although I myself had publicly burned my certificate when inaugurating the policy, I was left alone. Other people who could not produce identity certificates were manhandled and in many cases then detained or imprisoned. Much property belonging to villagers was taken away, immovable furniture was destroyed, and a good number of villages completely razed to the ground.

During all these disturbances about fifty of our people were shot dead.

Through all these happenings not a single member of the police or security forces was killed. Our people responded incredibly well to our call for life regardless of provocation. There were men and women in authority and many missionaries, both black and white, who were in isolated positions and could have easily fallen prey to our people, had these lost control of themselves or had any murderous intentions. I think I should add that later I visited the areas in which my party members had destroyed bridges and blocked roads and asked why this had been done. The answer I received was: 'You have told us not to hit back at these people and the only way we could defend ourselves in this situation was by trying to keep them away from our villages.' This may not have been a very far-seeing reaction, but it is one with which I feel a great deal of compassion. It is only fair, however, to say that the government has alleged that U.N.I.P. members (banning of the Z.A.N.C. had resulted in the formation of the United National Independence Party) had started blocking roads before the shooting began. But when this inconsistency of evidence caused me to call for an independent inquiry led by a British High Court Judge, my request was refused by the Government. We were willing to have our allegations investigated by an impartial person; it appears that they were not.

My purpose in explaining our Northern Rhodesian experience at such length has been to make it clear that we have tried to tread the difficult road of non-violent resistance to oppression. I think that, considering the difficulties under which we have been forced to operate, our success in doing so has been remarkable, although I am aware that not every one of our supporters has resisted provocation at all times. Neither can we deny that thugs and hooligans have sometimes committed acts of which most of us strongly disapprove, yet which have been attributed to us. The horrible attack upon Mrs Burton and her two children is the most well known of these cases.

My Support for Non-Violent Techniques

Thus I have done two things which might appear to be inconsistent. I have preached and tried to put into practice non-violent methods of achieving just ends. And I have preached that a particular policy should be followed in another case even if this necessitated the use of military power.

Why have I done this? I have not done these two things (both of which I still believe to be correct) because I wish to use non-violence as an empiricism, to be practised only when it suits my purpose. I believe, first and foremost, in the dignity of man; in his right to life and to a life with honour in it.

The essence of the non-violent doctrines is the respect for human life, and there is no doubt at all that man does not want to have himself hurt by his fellow men. Therefore, despite the world's history of violent conflict, man has realized that large areas of agreement can be reached and maintained without violence once people are determined to do this. For example, we have the concept of the nation states, within which we expect differences of opinion to be settled without fighting. This does not mean that all the people in a nation state are of like mind. When you find two men, you find two methods of approach to any given problem, and in any large community the multifarious differences between the members may or may not crystallize into two opposing groups; even if they do, it does not follow that there will be violent conflict between these groups. Mankind prepares to settle his dispute without war. He resorts to violence only when he feels some vital interest is being endangered. As man's understanding of his society increases and thus his acceptance of his own part in it, so the chances of his resorting to attacks on his fellows are reduced. Peace in any individual society is maintained more by social pressure, by the common acceptance of certain standards of behaviour than by other means, and a free society is certainly moving to a position of equilibrium between all the forces within itself. It must be understood, however, that the existence of one supreme arbiter – the government and its forces – can within variable limits maintain a social structure in a position of this equilibrium without violence breaking out.

None the less, conflicts between individuals, between groups, and most of all between states, do continue. Sometimes these conflicts are due to a mutual misapprehension – a misunderstanding of the desires or intentions of the other side; or a suspicion of the good faith on the part of those with whom there is a disagreement. These things can cause war on a large or small scale. But where a spirit of non-violence permeates the attitudes of both parties concerned in the misunderstanding, there will be discussions of their differences, and then probably a settlement acceptable (although not necessarily liked) by both sides. Sometimes, however, one of the parties in a conference believes that it can get its way completely because of its superior strength and therefore refuses to talk or consider the desires of those who oppose their wishes. In some ways this is a classical colonial situation. Yet even at this level it is often possible for the purposes of the victorious power to be largely undermined if the conquered people refuse to co-operate, and have the individual strength to maintain their opposition.

Thus, in practical terms, the concept of non-violence can sometimes enable a satisfactory settlement of disputes without the destructiveness of physical battle, and in other circumstances this conception cannot be the effective method of conducting the conflict at all. But there is more to non-violent methods than this; there is a morality about it too. Its practice at all levels cultivates passions, understanding and tolerance – virtues necessary to man's life with his fellows and in the physical environment of the world. But, most of all, non-violent methods of action ensure that the conflict is a worth-while one. The sufferer in a passive resistance campaign is the man who undertakes it. In his decision to work for something through these means, he is, in effect, saying that he does not wish to bring pain on anyone else, but he requires his objective so badly that he is willing to hurt himself to get it.

There is, however, one serious limitation of non-violent passive resistance techniques as a practical method for settling disputes. For to be effective it must be possible for the self-immolation involved to attract the attention and conscience of the opponent, or of other interested parties. In matters of social justice this might mean all mankind, because humanity is indivisible. Therefore there are circumstances in which passive resistance will be inappropriate as a weapon for achieving desired ends.

This is a very obvious truism. In Northern Rhodesia we have been able to use passive resistance because the British political system allows oppressed peoples to appeal to the conscience of the common man. I find it easy to fly to London at any time to call a press conference, hold public meetings and in other ways embarrass the government which is in power in Britain by organizing public opinion against them. I do not say this is easy – if it were, passive resistance techniques would be unnecessary. But because the British claim to adhere to the political doctrines of equality and democracy, and because they operate these within certain limits, it is possible for me, on behalf of the people of Northern Rhodesia, to try and challenge them in their consciences. The position of a leader from Angola or Mozambique is however very different. If such a person should fly to Lisbon it is highly unlikely that he would be allowed to return to continue his political work! If he should go to the U.N. in New York and then return to his home area he would not be heard of again. An African leader from Portuguese colonies might as well wave a red rag to a bull as go to Lisbon for political demands, or indeed stand up publicly and announce his intention of organizing a party to end the inferior position in which his people live. In neither case is colonialism justified; but in one case the struggle against it may be able to be fought on a basis of non-violence, while in the other such techniques cannot succeed.

In the case of conflicts between nations, the applicability of non-violent methods will vary. If one, or both, of the nations concerned refuse to accept the non-violent approach, or cause it to be so protracted that it is obviously meaningless, then it is very difficult to avoid violent conflict. Under these circumstances war will continue, unless you have a supernational organization which can police the areas of conflict and then force its decisions. This is where the U.N. must come in.

This is then the reason for my statement calling on the Indian government to invade Goa. Even those who condemned Nehru's action did not believe that Goa was part of Portugal. Everyone accepts that India has been waiting since 1947 to end this outpost of colonialism within her country. Non-violent techniques were not operable. It is similar circumstances which have led to reports such as that heading this article. China and India are two equally big nations; India now finds that China is not in the habit of solving problems with her neighbours in the same way as India wishes to do, i.e. by discussion and negotiation. Must India give way?

A MATTER OF LIFE

A great danger to the modern world and all of us who live in it is in fact just this sort of conflict between major powers. We are in a situation where no one wants war and where everyone is preparing for it and terrified of it. The great threat of nuclear weapons is forcing a continuation of talking, and a constant resumption of negotiations which have broken down. Everyone of us is involved and must recognize this practice. Yet it would be unrealistic for us to demand or expect either Russia or America alone to disarm regardless of the military balance of power, when each is convinced that the main purpose of the other is to overthrow the whole basis of their society. None the less, a solution to this mutual fear and suspicion must be found – the weapons alone require this. We in Africa are naturally incensed when atomic or hydrogen weapons are tested on our continent. Yet we have no illusions that the fall-out from bombs tested by Russia or America will by-pass Africa. We are involved in this conflict and all our pressure must be used on both sides to force the respective governments to recognize their responsibilities to mankind. The Russian series of tests in 1961 and the American series in 1962 indicate that at present they both believe that we, the rest of the world, can be ignored. I believe that we in Africa must play our part in shattering this dual illusion, although our techniques will not always be the same for both. The political systems and approaches of the two sides are different. But although our techniques will not always be the same, the contribution of Africa to the rest of the world may well be that part which we play in forcing these two powers to stop playing with the basis of our existence, like children playing with matches in an oil refinery. In the meantime, too, we have an interest in seeing that this madness of the nuclear arms race does not spread. Britain, France and China may now, or very soon, be able to brandish their own hydrogen bombs in the faces of the world; such actions give them no safety, nor do they add one iota to their power in relation to the two giants.

All that such arms can do is to add to the danger in which we all live.

Conclusion

I do not believe that the present limitations in the practice of non-violence mean that it is of limited importance. On the contrary, I believe that it may be the most important social agent for the betterment of mankind that has ever been discovered. It accords with the teachings of all the world-known religious leaders, and those of the people who might be termed leaders of progressive thought. It is based on the twin concepts of equality and love between men. Indeed, it follows from this automatically, because when there is love between people there is no question of them murdering each other for something which might arise; they will instead make every attempt to solve their problems peacefully.

Yet the principles of non-violence follow from the teachings of love, so it assists them by its insistence on the importance of the individual. It is something which depends on the individual, and is in a sense exclusively an individual weapon. It therefore may have a place in any society. Every political leader, whether democratic or dictatorial, is a prisoner of many circumstances. Sometimes he has vested interests to deal with; military or party leaders, or he may be a slave to an ideology; all of these mean that the common man has no direct access or influence on his leader. In these conditions it is difficult for the leader not to get out of touch, and it may be that in such circumstances the principles of non-violent resistance have another part to play.

But none of this is certain. While it is true that extreme goodness and love is the most powerful force there is, yet few of us are yet capable of it in its extremity. We therefore do not know its potentialities, any more than we really know the power and the problems raised by non-violent passive resistance to oppression. It is therefore necessary that students of non-violence should undertake further philosophical and practical studies into the meaning and the effectiveness of these techniques, and the possibility of developing them into a way of life. We are accustomed to scientists spending time in laboratories; we must pursue the same habits when examining the potentialities of this social agent as when examining the potentialities of a chemical agent.

This is not a religious question. It is political, economic, social and spiritual. It brings man, as an individual living in society, back into the centre of things. Nothing is more necessary, for we are now in danger of getting so wrapped up in machines, organizations and plans that man who is the purpose of it all is treated like an instrument. Man must realize his own importance, both as an individual and as a member of society.

Yet now we are left with an apparently unending series of questions. Is it still within man's grasp to save himself from the dangerous weapons he has created? Is it possible for nations which hate and fear each other to come together and discuss their problems peacefully? Is it possible for individuals to stop dislocating each other's jaws by the use of fists? I can see only one answer which is in itself a question. Can the conscience of the common man be aroused to action by a realization of his own importance in relation to the totality of human activity? If this happens mankind will develop a new sense of direction and responsibility. But it can only happen if we can reach the conscience of the common man.

SALVADOR DE MADARIAGA

Don Salvador de Madariaga was born in 1886 at Corunna in Spain and is Hon. President of the International Liberal Union and Congress for Freedom of Culture. He is an Hon. Fellow of Exeter College, Oxford, and among many honours has been awarded the Jade-in-Gold of China, the White Lion of Czechoslovakia, the Aztec Eagle of Mexico. He is a Knight of the Grand Cross of Orders of the Spanish Republic and holds the Légion d'Honneur of France.

THERE is no other objective way of understanding political progress than as an evolution from government by force to government by consent. A country is the more advanced the less violence it needs for the ordinary running of its collective affairs and even for its critical periods, when a phase of its life gives way to another phase. A typical example is Great Britain, where not only the normal change over from Labour to Tory government or vice versa is effected without a single pane being as much as scratched in the country, but where as profound a sociological revolution as that which began in 1914 and is still going on is taking place in perfect internal peace.

Since this way of understanding progress is grounded on the rule of law, the issue of disobedience to the law as a moral issue would at first sight seem idle. Disobedience to the law is a form of violence. It is therefore regressive. This conclusion, however, must be carefully qualified.

It is all very well to assert that we must obey the law. But whose law? What if the law itself is a form of violence? As a first approximation to a solution of this thorny problem, a distinction might be suggested between legitimate law and illegitimate law. Legitimate law must be obeyed. Illegitimate law need not be obeyed, and might even have to be disobeyed.

Our problem now has shifted to one of discovering a criterion to tell legitimate from illegitimate law. Here again we may seek a first approximation: legitimate can only be a law freely accepted by the freely organized institutions of the community to which it applies. This means that the community in question is governed by its own public opinion.

It follows that, provided a community is ruled by its public opinion, civil disobedience amounts to violence, and is therefore regressive.

Yet, even now we find on reflection that our conclusion stands in need of both clarification and qualification. Clarification, first. The statement that the rule by public opinion is the basis of a true democracy presupposes that this public opinion is free, spontaneous and well informed. Were this not so, the legitimacy of the law would evidently not be established. It seems plain, therefore, that it is open to any citizen to raise the question of the legitimacy of the law on this particular, purely institutional ground.

Does this justify civil disobedience? There is no prefabricated answer to this question. It seems that, within the four corners of a hypothetical situation such as that described here, there is room for seeking to improve matters by discussion; and that, if such is the case, civil disobedience would not be justified. If, however, the situation gave rise to no hope of betterment by discussion, or in cases of urgency, the dissentient citizen would find himself before a moral problem. He would have to decide whether his unfavourable judgment on the working of public opinion in his country was to prevail over that of the vast majority of his countrymen. I do not say it shouldn't. I say that it takes a tremendous faith in one's own judgment to believe that it must, and that there is here a risk of arrogance and therefore of error. This, however, is a caution, not a bar to action. It merely appeals to the free responsibility of the free citizen. That is all.

Once he has decided that he is right and the majority wrong, the dissident citizen has still to examine whether civil disobedience is the best or the only way to mend matters. He must be fully conscious of a number of reasons which would counsel prudence; for instance: that, in its very core, civil disobedience is regressive, even if in the case in question its immediate effects might in fact be progressive; or that what he does today, with his first-rate intellect and his pure heart, may be imitated tomorrow by duller brains and darker hearts. If he can pass over all these hurdles unfettered by his conscience, let him disobey.

So much for the clarification. Now, the qualification. A public opinion may be free, spontaneous and well informed and yet hopelessly wrong. It is a sad, disquieting, but indisputable fact that public opinion may go astray, indeed berserk. The ways it can err are so varied, the form and the gravity of the errors may differ so much, that, here again, the citizen is left to his own resources (subject to what I may have to say later on this precise point). There are cases too obvious to doubt. The world is unfortunately familiar with many, owing to relatively recent Nazi and communist abominations, events if any which ought to have given forth abundant crops of civic disobedience. But in probably the majority of cases the issue will raise every one of the points outlined above under 'clarification'. Am I sure my judgment is right? Is it not arrogant of me to be so sure of being right when so many people, many of them able, dissent from me? Even if I am right, is civil disobedience the best way out? But it does not follow that the citizen who ends this examination by going boldly for disobedience is necessarily wrong.

It would nevertheless seem advisable in any case for any citizen of a free country not to plunge into civil disobedience without an exhaustive inquiry, a widespread seeking of advice, and a persistent and patient recourse to the usual ways a true liberal democracy leaves open for a change of heart. The advice of other men recognized as disinterested and wise might be perhaps the most important step in this procedure. The sharpest intellect may be induced into error by a passionately held conviction whose very heat would deflect the otherwise straight rays of his vision. A strongly held view may lead to narrowing the field of vision and to twisting the object seen. Minority views are often the heralds of progress. This they achieve when they are not merely freaks but precursors. In such a case they are sure to appeal to at least a good number of wise and disinterested observers. To solicit the advice of such men would be prudent in any case; it becomes indispensable if a step as grave as civil disobedience is contemplated.

So, in the last analysis, the issue remains undecided; and the individual citizen cannot seek refuge in a hard-and-fast rule of behaviour. This is as it should be. The nobility of man's life is in his liberty and that of his liberty in his responsibility; and that of his responsibility in the originality of his every deed. Thus every minute of a free man's life is endowed with creative energy; and that is why freedom is to history what air is to life.

ODD NANSEN

Odd Nansen was born at Oslo in 1901 and is by profession an architect. From 1936 to 1952 he worked unceasingly for refugees and victims of the war in his own country and in Germany. He is special consultant to the Director General of UNESCO on German problems and a member of the board of the Norwegian Refugee Council. President of the Norwegian Section of the World Movement for World Government, he was elected Chairman of the Executive Committee for World Refugee Year in 1960.

As the last war drew to a close, when no one doubted any longer what would be its outcome, a number of prisoners were sitting in a German concentration camp discussing the problems and tasks which would have to be tackled when the war was over.

For a time the discussion proceeded at a high level, at any rate as high as might be expected among people who for years had lived in a hell on earth, surrounded by and undoubtedly influenced by devils.

All of a sudden the tone of the conversation dropped; the little group was now discussing what ought to be Hitler's fate once the war was over – and the debate now degenerated into an orgy of revenge. Each man vied with his neighbour in inventing the worst possible punishment, which this man so richly deserved.

Suggestions poured forth from the hidden recesses of the subconscious, one outdoing the other in refined sadism and cruelty. One had the impression that these suggestions had been lying, already fully developed, in the depths of men's minds, beneath an apparently innocent surface, and only needed the prompting of one word to gush out, like pus from a festering sore.

I have no intention of repeating more than one of these suggestions, actually the only one which can decently be repeated. It came from one of the prisoners after he had been sitting for some time in silence, listening to the others.

'I really believe,' he declared thoughtfully, 'that the worst possible punishment for this man, worse than the most refined torture, would be to equip him with a heart and a conscience – and compel him to continue to live with them.'

There were no further suggestions; the unplumbed depths of the subconscious closed their cavernous doors; a remark had been made which had silenced them instantaneously.

A MATTER OF LIFE

It was as though a gentle spring breeze, blowing from quite a different quarter of the human mind, had swept through the room, blotting away the poisonous fumes of an atmosphere which even hardened concentration camp inmates occasionally found difficult and distressing to believe.

A derisive commentary from one of the prisoners to this 'sentimental' suggestion was hardly uttered before it died in the silence – giving way on reflection to something else. Tacitly everyone agreed that the punishment which involved neither bloodshed nor physical torture was the worst of all.

Was it the fairest? Hardly. Judged by our yardstick of justice, which has been adapted to changing ages and generations, it would be tantamount to a verdict of not guilty. But judged by a higher, immutable, but perhaps unattainable yardstick of justice, it was clearly the severest.

My object in recounting this little episode from a distant and tragic past is not to suggest that a punishment of this kind would be right and reasonable for example in the case of Eichmann.

I simply wish to emphasize the great power of redemption that exists in those two nodal points of the ordinary man – the *heart* and the *conscience*. If we include the *reason*, our trio will be complete. Surely this triple combination is the strongest and most enduring in a man's life and development on earth?

The punishment itself is of no interest: it can seldom provide a basis on which anything of real value can be built. After all, it comes after the misdeed – or the catastrophe – has occurred. It should therefore only be of interest to the legal expert. True enough, in his sentence the judge should at all times – in order to ensure law and order, as the saying goes – have due regard for public opinion. His sentence should not violate what is called 'the people's own sense of justice', which is really nothing less than a synonym for the people's thirst for revenge. As a rule revenge takes no account whatever of the responsibility which must be borne by the people themselves for the fact that the crime actually took place.

One word more about Eichmann: he has been made the scapegoat for one of the greatest and most terrible crimes ever committed in the history of mankind. Although he undoubtedly played a decisive and focal role in the execution of this crime, obviously no one really believes that a single person can be made responsible for the murder of an entire people, a murder which was planned, administered, and systematically carried out over a number of years with satanic cold-bloodedness.

The thousands – or tens of thousands – who were directly implicated, large or small cog-wheels in the actual machinery of crime, were not the only guilty ones; their guilt must be shared by the nation who allowed this foul deed to be done!

The verdict of guilty must also be brought in against an age which closed its eyes, and allowed this nation, led by a gang of desperate criminals, to pursue its evil path until it was too late to hinder its monstrous crimes against humanity.

If Eichmann – or his collaborators – had individually adopted an attitude of civil or ethical disobedience, refusing to sully their hands with this evil work, they would undoubtedly have been shot. There is equally no doubt that others would have taken their places in the murder machine and carried out the same programme.

As long as the death penalty is established in law, and that murder remains a laudable national act, there will never be any lack of executioners, passive or active, it matters little which. One might be tempted to say that the passive ones are the worst: they are at any rate the most dangerous, because they are more numerous and have a greater say. They have no heart, they have no conscience, they have no reason. They are devoid of all those qualities required for civil disobedience or any form of reaction against evil. They are the victims of the most dread plague of our age – *indifference*, whose outstanding symptoms are egocentric materialism and mental impotence.

Once a criminal impotence of this kind envelops a whole nation, anything can happen – not only in Germany. What might not happen if it spread and covered the whole world?

We must in fact train our spotlight on the nations themselves. Only if they are capable jointly of reacting against evil, and willing to defend their cultural values and their human dignity against the powers of destruction, will it be possible to prevent similar catastrophes.

The natural human mass reaction against the inhuman laws which 'legalize' crime, or the *mass campaign* to remove them, never materialize. Neither in Germany nor in any other country. Not, at any rate, until it is too late.

Why?

Why? Why? How many humiliating questions of this kind must we answer?

But have we no answer?

We were not involved; so it was not *our* affair. But fellow human beings in extreme need, calling for our help, were involved. Was it not our duty to help?

It was too late to help them.

Could we not have made the effort?

It would have been ridiculously naïve to believe that unarmed public opinion, guided by something as sentimental as love of one's neighbour, would have had any influence whatsoever on an established, totalitarian régime, based on a police force and on military power, and inspired by a ruthless contempt for human dignity.

But if public opinion had grown up *before* the régime had been established – before a point was reached when it was too late – would love of one's neighbour then have had any chance of overcoming inhumanity?

It *was* already too late, when we saw what was happening and realized what was happening.

ODD NANSEN

Did we merely shut our eyes, to avoid seeing and understanding? Hoping, perhaps, that *we* might escape the holocaust?

Any other course would have been perilous.

But what about all our great ideas about liberty, fraternity and equality? Are they no longer worth anything, and do they mean so little that we can conveniently dismiss them whenever our lives are threatened?

We have other duties – we have our wives and children.

And yet – there were some, quite a few, who placed their ideals higher than life itself, men who without hesitation, though they knew it would cost them their lives, exerted all their strength and ability, all the force of their conviction, all their enthusiasm and love in the task of constructively helping their fellow men, and who without compromise fought for freedom, justice and human dignity, against suppression and terror, until they met their deaths in battle or beneath the executioner's axe.

What was the use of their struggle?

More than anything else it was thanks to their efforts, to their struggle, and their deaths, that the highest ideals of our civilization somehow survived the holocaust that followed. Surely that was worth life and struggle?

We needed our armaments and our defences ourselves – should the need arise. And it did.

Thus, vainly hoping that we should save ourselves, as long as possible, we proved untrue to our own convictions, to our own conscience, and to the fundamental ideas of our civilization, only to be dragged into the conflict between good and evil, resulting in a slaughter unparalleled in the history of the world.

* * *

And yet the most terrible thing about war is after all not the bloodshed; it is not the suffering and the loss of human lives. We must all die some day, innocent and guilty alike. Happy is the man who dies innocent, or fighting for the things that are dear to him.

The most terrible thing about war is the moral defeat which makes it possible – and the period of degradation that follows in its wake, the consummation of defeat which we all suffered, victors and vanquished alike; and then the stinging and inevitable truth that we learnt *nothing*! That peace is further away than ever before! That all sense of brotherhood and fellow feeling seems to have been blotted out from the face of the earth. That lust for power, distrust and self-interest determine relations between nations and people – while the masses are sunk in apathy and indifference.

Without even raising our voices in protest, we have all been indifferent witnesses to the fate of three small Baltic nations swallowed up one after the other by a powerful neighbour, and wiped off the face of the map.

Without lifting a finger we have watched as one country after another has been enslaved and silenced by foreign tyranny.

We watched the Hungarians rise to a man in a struggle for their freedom and human rights against their brutal oppressors. It was no concern of ours; Suez and our oil interests were at stake.

But the unanswered, heart-rending appeal of the Hungarians to the outside world for help in their struggle against the tyrant has placed a heavy and uneasy burden on our frayed conscience, and made it more difficult for us to look one another in the eye.

When Tibet was attacked, robbed and plundered, we averted our gaze.

Oppression and discrimination against coloured people in South Africa and elsewhere are allowed to proceed unhindered, now as before. The small and the weak people of this world are kept in subjection, now as before. We close our borders to the countless refugees, now as before; we close our eyes to their sufferings and distress, until it is too late to save them.

That over two-thirds of the population of the world should be living at or below the starvation level is equally of little concern to us today – now as before.

What a disgrace, what an ineradicable stain on the civilization to which we belong, whose highest commandment is love of one's neighbour.

The call of the Hungarians, the stifled cries of the oppressed, the silent prayer of starving people for help, these cannot be met with civil disobedience alone. That would be giving a stone for a loaf of bread.

Let us never forget that when all our problems have been weighed and every approach rejected, when the prospect is unrelieved darkness, there is still faith, hope and charity; and the greatest of these is charity. It is charity, or love – more than anything else – to which these appeals are made. Love of one's fellow men translated into constructive action; when all is said and done, acts of charity are more effective than all the protests in the world.

We protest and demonstrate with bands and banners – providing the newspapers with excellent copy for a while. We hand out peace prizes (how cynical), we hold peace congresses (what tragicomedies), we organize, we celebrate, and we arrange. No one could possibly accuse us of not ventilating our views. After all, we are free men and women!

But we fail to act. The organized, co-ordinated, constructive mass action, which aims to put right what everyone in the world – if they were asked – would agree is so utterly wrong, *that* particular action never materializes.

I am afraid that it never will – and that wrongs will never be righted as long as people's reaction to these wrongs is confined to civil or ethical disobedience, sporadic protests, strikes, or whatever we prefer to call them, alone.

As long as demonstrations of this kind retain the glamour and attraction of a sensation, they may well fire the imagination for a brief while, and rouse some of those who are slumbering. They might even lead to immediate results, with which one is so easily satisfied before the cares of every day and the sense of all-pervading indifference once again swallows them up. But I do not believe that they will ever produce results of lasting value on which a new and better future can be built.

They are bought too cheaply.

There is an ancient and inherent strain of disobedience in all men and women – not only in children who are loath to obey their parents, but also in adults we find this desire to avoid irksome duties. Sometimes all that is required is a *no* and a signature. This is sufficient to give one peace, and the confident feeling that 'others' will do the rest. That is, if one really believes that something should be done.

A highly respected and upright citizen in my country put his name to a resolution protesting *against* nuclear weapons. Everyone respected him for that. Later on there was a campaign *in favour* of nuclear weapons, and forgetting for a moment that he had already put his name to a contrary resolution, he was asked to give his support to this latest campaign. 'I should like to have supported this resolution,' he replied, 'if I hadn't already put my name to the protest resolution.' He did at any rate remember the document to which he had appended his name. This simple little story is perhaps not so devoid of meaning as it sounds. Both campaigns sought to promote the same goal: peace on earth. There was disagreement on the means of achieving this. The poor man was actually in doubt himself – and might well have signed both resolutions with an equally good conscience.

With all due respect to the idealism and the excellent intentions which undoubtedly in the case of a great many people – though alas all too few – provide the motive for disobedience of this kind and protests of this nature, by their very nature they are inevitably *negative*, unless the strength of their conviction and their force are so great that they find expression in a constructive programme, with constructive solutions of the problems involved.

A defective wheel in a machine must be replaced by a new one if the machine is to function satisfactorily. If the whole machine is defective, obsolete, or completely unsuited for its purpose, a new one must be designed and built. Protesting against the old machine is not enough. But it is so much easier. It costs so much less work and trouble. Besides, God knows whether it will be any use!

The masses cannot build a new machine. But if a machine of this kind is built – and if the masses were convinced that it would serve their interests to have it – then they could assist in building it. In fact, without their help it would perhaps never be possible to build it.

When we realize how amazingly simple it is to enlist the support of the masses for something that is utterly wrong – especially if it appeals to their worst instincts, and the appeal of personal gain is involved – and when we realize that they can be persuaded to join in protests and strikes *against something patently wrong*, then surely it should be possible to rally them in a mass campaign in *favour of something that is so patently right* – especially when this *something* is a matter of to be or not to be? I almost said, even though it appealed to their best instincts and qualities.

To the extent that we are capable of creating this 'something that is so patently right', in face of the overhanging problem of today; in other words, an international set-up capable of excluding war and securing peace – and to the extent that we are capable of getting the masses to understand the advantage to themselves and to all their fellow men of building this machine, we have a chance of continuing to exist on this planet of ours.

* * *

A MATTER OF LIFE

Little imagination is required to realize that the latest technological and scientific achievements – nuclear fission – have introduced a new and entirely revolutionary epoch in the history of mankind. It is capable of perverting the normal development of all life on earth, of upsetting all traditional ways of thinking, and bringing disharmony into our existence. It offers far-reaching perspectives and possibilities for good and evil, whose full scope we cannot yet foresee and yet which fill us with unspeakable dread.

One thing at any rate is certain: only a short time ago, after this tremendous new source of power had been made known, we realized that if used in the service of destruction – and it was for this purpose that it was first used – it is capable today of extinguishing all life on this earth.

This possibility alone, far exceeding the grasp of most people, puts it beyond the control of the human mind, whose dazzling achievement it was. What devilish irony, what senseless tragedy, if one of the greatest triumphs of the human spirit were to lead to the destruction of mankind! Hundreds of years before its time, a frontier was crossed which we now wish had remained closed until man was prepared to cross it.

This frontier can no longer be closed, however vociferously we protest. Knowledge, once acquired, cannot be forgotten. There is no use running away from it, or from the problems it raises. We have personally created these problems, and we must face them. No one can say that he does not know them, for they are available to all. Any scientist, soldier or politician, any enlightened person we meet on our road, can tell.

And then we protest against the use of nuclear power in the service of destruction: nuclear armaments! Of course! I should like to see the person, east or west of the Iron Curtain, who would not be prepared to protest against the self-destruction which the use of this weapon would involve. Everybody, whether they live in the East or the West, whether they are communist or capitalist, Christian or non-Christian, coloured or white, has one thing in common: they want to live. Of course they rise in protest and in self-defence against everything and everybody threatening to deprive them of life.

And now nuclear weapons are involved.

But what about the other weapons? The V1, V2, blockbusters, and all the others? During the second World War hundreds of thousands of people were wiped out in the course of a few days by these engines of destruction. What about chemical and biological methods of destruction, which today, with a never-ceasing devilish inventiveness, have been developed to a point where they are perhaps no less destructive than nuclear arms? Are they to be 'permitted', and to be tucked away under the label of 'conventional weapons', which are not so 'dangerous'?

If we protest against a particular weapon, and demand that it should be abolished, do we not tacitly accept the others? As though they were not, all of them, death-dealing. Is it the degree of terror against which we are protesting, or is it mass murder? Or self-destruction? Are we aiming at a 'humanization' of war? What an absurd idea, that warfare could ever be 'humanized'.

Is not it war itself against which we should protest? War as a means of solving disputes between nations and peoples?

Supposing the protests were effective! Supposing an international agreement was actually achieved, that is to say, an agreement between East and West banning the manufacture and use of nuclear weapons – and the destruction of all extant stocks of atom bombs. Is there anyone who really believes that this would mean the abolition of war?

Supposing war broke out none the less? Does anyone really believe that East and West would have forgotten how to produce atom bombs? Does anyone really believe that the international agreement would prevent East – or West –

from manufacturing them – and using them – if either one party or the other considered this to be to its advantage?

Poison gas was not used in the second World War. Not because of the ban in the Hague Convention against its use, but because each side knew that if it used it, then the poison gas would immediately be used against it.

If I may be permitted a brief aside, I should like to mention one of the clauses in the Hague Convention. It still contains an almost touching little ban on the use of so-called dum-dum bullets in time of war. I expect only a few people know today what a dum-dum bullet is: it is a rifle bullet of small calibre, the outer metal covering of which is pierced in front, with the result that the lead core expands on impact with a human – or animal – body, causing laceration and terrible wounds.

The very ban on the use of this projectile, which was at one time regarded as the most diabolic of all, reveals two factors that are worth noting: an acceptance of war; and a sort of romantic evaluation of what is fair and what is unfair when it comes to killing one's enemies. As though considerations of this kind have anything whatever to do with modern warfare!

But who would worry about the bans and the rules of the Hague Convention if they proved an obstacle to one's plans in time of war? Who would worry about non-aggression pacts and other solemn international agreements, if it served their purpose to violate them? Would they not all be mere scraps of paper, worth no more than Germany's guarantee of Belgian neutrality in 1914? Who could stop – or punish – the guilty party?

Despite the laudable regulations of the Hague Convention, the Italians used poison gas against more or less unarmed Abyssinians in 1936. The Germans used it against defenceless Jews during the rising in the Warsaw Ghetto in 1943, and in the liquidation centres in their concentration camps throughout the war. This was done because in neither of these cases was there the slightest reason to fear retaliation!

In other words, fear was the decisive factor in deciding whether to use or not to use outlawed weapons. Not the fear of violating the rules of the Hague Convention, but the fear of retaliation! The fear of being the victim of one's own devilment, which one would otherwise have no scruples in inflicting on innocent fellow men in enemy countries.

The terror that struck Hiroshima and Nagasaki – only a cautious anticipation of what was to come – would never have taken place if the Japanese had been in possession of nuclear arms. Just how long the war would have lasted – and how many people would have been killed with conventional weapons – is another question.

All this, and a great deal besides that we have seen and experienced in our barbaric age, leads us to the logical conclusion that it is fear of a modern war which, at any rate at the moment, is the most effective means of preventing it breaking loose. The worse it appears to our underdeveloped imagination, the more we fear it!

If this conclusion is correct – and I cannot with the best of intentions see how it could be otherwise – then in the name of peace let us ensure that war is as frightful as possible.

But fear is an unsatisfactory yardstick, ethically, morally and in practice, and it is certainly a useless foundation for enduring peace. But what makes it possible for me to accept it, at any rate to a certain extent, is that it is so blessedly human. Although in its naked helplessness it is perhaps not one of our proudest or noblest qualities, it is nevertheless closely bound up with the good, life-proclaiming forces within us.

Provided it does not rob us of all our strength, and degenerate into panic terror – or apathy – and remains subordinate to heart, conscience and reason, it should be possible to convert it into a co-ordinated constructive effort for peace. But work of this kind must be carried out irrespective of all boundaries – ideological as well as geographical, political and religious – and the masses must be informed of this work, they must gain confidence in its leaders, and they must believe that a road exists which will avoid catastrophe, provided we stand united in our endeavour to find that road.

There is every indication that today, with two giant powers in the East and in the West menacing the world with their armaments, and with the abyss yawning at our feet, fear – and for the time being nothing but fear – alone gives us a chance of postponing the catastrophe.

Everything will depend on how we utilize this chance! *One* thing is certain: we have not much time left!

* * *

Some people believe that the only road to peace is through each person's conversion to God. A great deal of noble self-effacing work is carried out to achieve this purpose.

But one may well ask: which God?

If it is the God of the Christians, this would mean that of the approximately three and a half milliard people who inhabit the earth, well over two milliard will first have to be converted.

Even if it were only a question of converting half this number or even less, and even if we worked with redoubled energy, using all our faith and sincere hope, we have no time to wait so long. Patience may be a splendid quality, but there are situations where impatience is preferable. I believe we are in a situation of that kind.

'Religion ... is the opium of the people,' said Marx.

I am not prepared to subscribe to this categorical and heathen statement, but I should simply like to point out that it *may* contain a grain of truth. A confession – or a propaganda – which aims to persuade people, especially when they fear for their existence, that everything will turn out for the best provided they turn to God, believe in Him, and place everything in His hands, is dangerous and harmful.

ODD NANSEN

Perhaps it is the most harmful of all; it can certainly be compared with opium.

In the profoundest sense of the word it is also un-Christian and immoral, because it is introvert and teaches that every human being, no matter what situation he is in, should first and foremost concentrate on himself and his own salvation. As though it were the most important of all, when a whole world is tottering on the brink of the abyss. As though one's own salvation did not in fact entail obeying the command of love: *forget yourself*!

'Good deeds will save the world,' said a great Norwegian poet, Bjørnstjerne Bjørnson, on his deathbed. It was as though, in a last moment of visionary clarity, he discerned the greatest truth and put it into simple words. Words which summed up his own life's work and experience. A life in the service of freedom, human dignity, justice, and love of humanity.

The longer I live, and the more I see of people in despair and distress, and of people enjoying superabundance and contentment, the more convinced I have been that he was right, and that his last message to us has eternal validity.

Good deeds must lead the way and prepare the crusade for peace which will have to come, and to which all people must rally, if we are to survive. Good deeds by us who live on the sunny side to help those who live in the shadows.

I seem to hear a chorus of voices raised in the well-known cry: charity begins at home!

Yes, that is so. Love of one's neighbour begins at home, as does everything of value in life. But it mustn't end there, too.

It is not a question of where it begins, but how far it extends. Today nothing extends far enough unless it reaches right the way round the world. And what is needed is not alms or charity: not the crumbs that fall from the rich man's table, but the right to sit at his table, and to partake in his meal, without feeling humiliated.

A MATTER OF LIFE

What the world needs is good deeds which aim to obliterate the crying injustice of hundreds of millions of people exploited and oppressed materially and intellectually by a dominant minority – deeds which aim to bridge the yawning chasm between poor and rich, between the hungry and the well-fed.

Don't imagine for a moment that it is of any use talking to a starving person about anything but food. Years of experience among people of this kind have taught me that hunger is capable of reducing men and women to the level of primitive animals, where practically all human qualities have given way to an animal desire for food – food.

The horrifying fact that two-thirds of the population of the world are starving – or living on the edge of starvation – provides an obvious indication of the way in which we must set to work if we are to raise these milliards, on whom our own future and the future of the world depends, out of their misery, so that they can take their place as normal fellow humans with whom we can talk reason.

I seem to hear another chorus of statistical know-alls talking of the problem of over-population, insisting that so-and-so many millions of people must die of starvation, disease, or war every year if we are to avoid a catastrophic over-population of the world. It is deplorable, they admit, but we simply must be careful not to interfere with the balance of nature which solves this problem for us – for a while, at any rate – so simply and so practically.

Such are the arguments put forward by a materialistic and pleasure-loving 'world upper class', in an attempt to justify their vested interests, and in order to ensure that they can still help themselves to the good things of this world, at the expense of the millions who are kept down consciously and ruthlessly – and are abandoned to the 'balance of nature'.

Apart from the fact that modern research has rejected these terrifying arguments as unfounded and untrue, it is hardly necessary to say anything more about the ethical and moral standards of those who use these arguments, when they should know better.

The fear of over-population of the earth has constantly recurred, ever since the English theologian Thomas Robert Malthus (1798) elaborated his gloomy theories that population figures increased far more rapidly than food production. Statistical investigations have repeatedly given the lie to this theory. It has been scientifically established that even with the increase in population that is taking place today (an increase that in all probability will fall off with the spread of information, higher standards of living, and an increased sense of social responsibility) there is room and food enough for the population of the earth, for an indefinite period in the future. By no means all the resources of the world, on land and at sea, have been exploited for food production, and a great deal of what is exploited (all too often wastefully) could yield many times more with modern methods.

We need only turn to the investigations carried out by the United Nations F.A.O. to discover that the conclusion reached is that food production is increasing more rapidly than population figures. In fact, according to the F.A.O. the main problem was actually to reduce various surplus stocks – without reducing prices!

This calls to mind the acute shortage of food in Russia after the first World War (1921-2). When this catastrophe was at its worst, with thousands of persons dying every day, from the other side of the Atlantic came the strange news, which made an indelible impression on me, that millions of tons of maize and wheat were being used for fuel or were being dumped in the sea, in the Argentine and the U.S.A., for lack of markets!

Or was it to maintain price levels? And we were informed that at that time there were three to four million tons of grain more in the world than the whole of mankind was capable of consuming, while over thirty million people – only a few days' journey away – were starving to death.

At the same time the bulk of the world's merchant navies was lying idle – laid up.

Is there a more illuminating example of the world's lack of kindliness, conscience and reason? Is it surprising that every man is all out for himself, that anxiety neuroses, mistrust of everything and everybody, and an unwillingness to co-operate, should spread in a world of this kind, where barriers between people are retained willy-nilly, while the distance between countries becomes shorter with every day that passes?

Only a blind man would fail to see that the world is daily becoming more and more of a unit, and – whether we like it or not – that we must accept the fact that we are all in the same boat, a situation which our own technical development has made inevitable. We must face this fellowship and act accordingly, as we have done in the various cultural communities.

Within each community the existence of every individual is secured by laws which guarantee us all work, and pay, and protect us against privation. A system of justice protects us against injustice and oppression, ensures law and order and industrial peace.

It is an offence in law to fail to render help to a fellow human in peril of his life, if we are capable of so doing. It is an offence to take the law into one's own hands, at the expense of others. It is an offence to disturb law and order, to prevent others carrying out their lawful occupations, let alone conspiring to take the life of someone else.

Within this system of law, justice and authority, which we all accept as a matter of course, the individual has an opportunity of realizing himself, his capabilities and his talents, so that he can develop in freedom but with responsibility. But without love of one's fellow men, without a sense of social responsibility and conscience, and without common sense, our cultural community is unthinkable. Without them the entire system would merely be a skeleton without flesh and blood.

After thousands of years of struggle and suffering, disappointment, victory and defeat, we have achieved this. We have got so far, but no further! For beyond national boundaries, in the world community, nothing of all this exists. Here the law of the jungle still holds good. Here might is still right. For this reason, too, it is not a cultural community. It is a lawless arena where injustice and the abuse of power have free play.

I can see no other solution – and no other escape from this caveman state of affairs – than the one which led to the creation and development of the various cultural communities. Lawlessness, the abuse of power, and injustice, must be replaced by law, authority, and justice.

In my opinion, it is futile to expect any real peace in the world, that is to say, the certainty that war will be excluded and rendered impossible as a means of solving disputes between groups of peoples or nations, without the establishment of an effective system of compulsory world justice, with world laws and with force to back those laws. This force, however, shall be limited in its task to the prevention of war.

This would involve the following: complete disarmament under effective international supervision (not merely a reduction or limitation of armaments); clear-cut laws against the use of force (applicable to nations and individuals alike); courts of justice to interpret and to apply these laws in all international disputes; a world police force, with careful safeguards to prevent its misuse, for the maintenance of these laws.

There is nothing new in this system. In our individual communities it is taken for granted. So much so that we no longer wonder what life would be without it.

'This is not realistic politics! This is Utopia!' the worldly-wise politicians will say, shaking their heads at the naïve, blue-eyed fools who really believe that theft, deception and murder could ever be forbidden by international law. As though it were possible for thieves, swindlers and murderers to be brought to book and punished in the world community, too!

But what *is* realistic policy?

Does it mean offering hard-boiled, political and ideological programmes to a suffering, terrified humanity? Waving a palm of peace – and a loaf – in one outstretched hand, while the other – holding an atom bomb – is adroitly concealed behind one's back! And all this time the world is sliding nearer and nearer to the abyss.

Yes, alas! That seems to be the realistic policy of today! But it is the realistic policy of Satan, leading to the destruction of mankind. Never has the Prince of Darkness had better cards in his hand! Never has he been closer to the fulfilment of his diabolical desires!

Perhaps we can't see him? Perhaps we don't realize that he is an active agent – a satanic demon – strategically placed in the subconscious of every single human being, exploiting every moment of weakness in the conscious world to drive us to devilment. For its own sake!

Let me admit that during the period I spent in a German concentration camp during the last war there were times when this demon was so much a reality that I could literally see him as large as life in front of me. I fought with him every single day – and it was a life-and-death struggle. I know that if I had not fought I shouldn't be here today, talking about the road to peace on earth, trying to express my conviction that there is another form of political reality than the one that appears to rule the roost today.

After all, what is Utopia?

'A fantastic ideal state. The most perfect political, social, and legal state or condition. A figment of the imagination,' according to my dictionary.

Let me attempt another definition:

Utopia is the description which any age gives to all the great pioneering ideas that have enabled humanity to move forwards and upwards.

Let our programme, then, be Utopian. Never mind whether people call us naïve and blue-eyed for believing it.

Let us admit our fear of total destruction, and our wish to live – in the belief that our life, despite all, has a meaning which we shall one day have an opportunity of discovering.

Let us openly admit that we have not yet lost all our faith in the good in men. That we still believe firmly and entirely that goodness is more effective and lasts longer than brute force.

We must not allow all our positive human qualities, all our love of life and our healthy reaction against evil, to peter out in a negative protest.

Let us go even further, and work ceaselessly to promote a common world-embracing mass campaign, aimed at establishing the system of law and justice that alone can raise the world community out of its state of barbarism and make it into a cultural community.

For this work, the most important work in the world, we shall need not least those qualities with which my fellow prisoner would have liked to have equipped Hitler – love and conscience. The third leaf in this trefoil – common sense – makes this human triple combination stronger than any other, stronger even than nuclear power.

Let this be the armour we shall put on in our crusade! But in the heat of the battle let us never forget that the greatest of these qualities is love.

JAWAHARLAL NEHRU

Jawaharlal Nehru was born in Allahabad in 1889. He became Barrister-at-Law at the Inner Temple in 1912. He was a member of the All India Congress Committee in 1918 and worked with Gandhi. He was imprisoned on several occasions for his political activities. He has been Prime Minister and Minister for External Affairs in India since 1947. His published works are many and varied and include several historical treatises.

*Prime Minister's House,
New Delhi.*

February 27, 1962.

Dear Mrs Urquhart,

I am sure that the book you are bringing out will be important and useful. But it is not clear to me how I can write anything worthwhile for this symposium.

Apart from the difficulty of finding time for it, I really do not think I am competent enough to deal with this subject. I have no doubt that on certain occasions disobedience of laws on ethical grounds may be justified. Indeed sometimes it may become the duty of a person to disobey and take the consequences of such disobedience. The question when such disobedience can be justified is one ultimately for the individual himself to answer. The very reason for this disobedience is that normally one should obey the laws, but when something happens which is objected to on ethical grounds which are valid, then the individual must judge which is better, to obey or to disobey.

This, in brief, is what I think on the subject.

Yours sincerely,

JAWAHARLAL NEHRU

SALVATORE QUASIMODO

Professor Salvatore Quasimodo was born at Syracuse in Sicily in 1901, and has been a Professor of Italian Literature at the Guiseppe Verdi Conservatory in Milan, since 1941.

In 1959 he was awarded the Nobel Prize for Literature. As a poet and critic he is of world standing and his translations of Shakespeare's works into the Italian language have been widely acclaimed.

At a moment like this it is clear that we are no longer dealing with social problems; polemicizing on wealth or poverty: the H-bomb threatens the earth and its highest aspirations.

The man of science, or the man against science; the fisherman who sails round Bikini, or even five thousand miles away from the atoll, knows how life on this earth is going to finish – or could finish. At those very margins where the soil begins to rise up from the atoll, even as it pulses with vegetation and living forms it knows the disintegration of matter. Volcanic ash once constituted a primeval threat to the forces of nature and man-made radioactivity may indeed overthrow the powers of nature – but nevertheless will not shake nature herself.

Man has reached the limits of his destructive powers; undreamed of by any 'superman'. Tomorrow there will not be any judges or judged left. And those religious precepts of punishment or reward in what lies beyond will lack any point of reference, when there is no continuation of life on the earth from which these ideas sprang.

Science and intellect have created the perfect weapon with which to commit their own suicide, at the same time causing the murder of all living cells, and have put this weapon into the hands of soldiers. Intelligence must now fight – and it will fight to prevent this monstrous robot from being brought to life.

Poets, artists, writers can all fight and they must fight, trusting in the humanitarian ideals that alone are capable of recalling men to sanity once more. Indifference and apathy have only one name – betrayal.

HERBERT READ

Sir Herbert Read was born in 1893 at Muscoates Grange, Kirbymoorside, Yorkshire, and educated at Crossley's School, Halifax, and the University of Leeds. He is President of the Society for Education through Art, the Institute of Contemporary Arts and the British Society of Aesthetics. He is also a member of the Académie Flamande des Beaux Arts and the Académie Royale des Beaux Arts, Stockholm. His many publications on visual arts, and on the art of poetry and prose, include: *Art and Society*, and *A Concise History of Modern Painting*.

I

CIVIL disobedience is a phrase with a long and respectable history – I suppose Henry Thoreau first established it in a famous essay which he wrote in 1849. But admittedly it is not a very precise phrase, for to obey or disobey implies the previous issue of a command. If a country's laws are regarded as a set of such commands, then the thief or the murderer is committing an act of civil disobedience.

But that was not Thoreau's conception of civil disobedience, nor even Gandhi's. Nor is the conception of civil disobedience of those who have now decided that civil disobedience is the only way out of the fearful impasse of politics.

We, the citizens of this country, are not commanded to use nuclear weapons. If we are to believe our politicians, the use of these weapons will be decided by the Prime Minister and his military advisers; but even this is not certain, for in an emergency a decision may have to be taken by the officer in charge of a missile base, or a submarine, who may not even be a British subject. In any case, those few people who will decide the matter are at present dependent on a system of warnings which by reason of its mechanical nature cannot be absolutely free from the possibility of a breakdown. Accidents will happen.

The use or non-use of nuclear weapons is a complex issue, which in any given situation involves uncertain factors, of responsibility and of decision. Moreover, the 'given situation' is not a future state of alarm or a threat of aggression: it is the present existence and constant deployment (by aeroplane and submarine) of a large and increasing stockpile of annihilating weapons.

So long as the bombs exist, in their hundreds and perhaps already their thousands, the detonation of one or more, by

A MATTER OF LIFE

accident or design, is a mathematical probability. I believe that sober mathematicians, calculating all the risks, would conclude, not a probability but a certainty. The risks increase as the stock of bombs increases and is multiplied by the number of nations possessing these bombs.

According to some atomic scientists there is now a ray of hope in this mad race for more and bigger bombs. A missile has been invented – the American solid-fuel Minute-man – which is at once so powerful and so dispersable that no nation will ever take the certain risk of self-destruction by provoking its use. The present strategy, designed for fixed missile bases, is dependent on precise time signals. In the future such precision timing will not be necessary because bombs of deterrent strength will be deployed over wide areas and will therefore cease to be fixed and predestined targets.

The new strategy, flexible in itself, aims at a permanent condition of universal stalemate. The world, divided into two camps, is to remain for ever deadlocked in mutual terror. Instead of the Sword of Damocles, the Minute-man will hang over our heads. But the point of the legend of Damocles is that he was not able to enjoy the felicity offered to him under such conditions. Nor could the world enjoy felicity under a similar threat. Damocles could not avoid the sight of the suspended sword that destroyed happiness; the world might not see the hidden Minute-men, but it could not forget their existence, and there would be plenty of 'minor incidents', and indeed major crises such as the one that has now arisen over Berlin, to remind us of this ultimate and irrevocable sanction.

As a human being who believes that in spite of all its inherent absurdity life on this planet has some obscure purpose, and even on the foundation of his inevitable sufferings could be made pleasurable for man, I cannot regard a permanent threat of universal destruction with equanimity.

I am now too old to worry much about the remnant of my

own life, and in a situation like the one I am discussing I do not particularly distinguish between the lives of my own children and the lives of the children of other people. I do not particularly distinguish between British lives and Russian lives, American or Chinese lives. It is life itself and what we make of it (which is civilization) that is threatened.

Threatened by whom? It is when one asks this question that the absurdity of the situation becomes clear. It is certainly not a threat made by the British *people*, nor by the American, or Russian, or Chinese *people*: people all over the world (and I speak from the experience of direct contact with the Chinese and Russian, as well as the American and British people) are very much the same. Their material needs are much the same, their ideals of comfort and of good living, their spiritual aspirations.

They differ outrageously in standards of living, but there is no reason at all (as J. D. Bernal and other scientists have shown) why these inequalities, which may be a reason for envy and mistrust, should not be resolved by peaceful means. The trouble between nations is created by ideologists and politicians, aided and encouraged by the armed forces, the churches, and the press. I don't know what to call this complex of power addicts: it is wider than the 'Establishment' in any country, and it is wider than the 'Government'. Though the government of a country is the 'head' of this complex animal, its body is amorphous. It is indeed invisible, and it is invisible because it is hidden below ground, in the collective unconscious.

This concept, common to Freudians and Jungians however differently they may name it, implies that every individual mind is partly occupied by tendencies to instinctive reaction that belong to the community as a whole, perhaps to the whole human race. I do not intend to detail the evidence for this hypothesis – psychoanalysis has accumulated a vast amount of it, and it is inescapable. But assuming the existence of these unconscious collective forces which drive us towards mutual extermination, how can we deal with them?

The answer is: we must first get acquainted with them. They are demons which can be exorcized only by self-knowledge, and by the cultivation of good demons to take their place – that is to say, impulses of mutual aid and universal brotherhood. But in order to get acquainted with our bad demons, and to replace them by good demons, we need to generate the kind of mass emotions that have characterized the great religious movements in the past. Some of those movements have gone astray, and more often than not the good collective emotions generated at the beginning of them have been perverted by unscrupulous leaders. But that must not deter us. The Christian pilgrimages failed because they were conceived in military terms: the means were evil and infected the ends. Gandhi's means were not evil and the ends were realized without distortion.

Naturally, mass movements will not achieve miracles. In the end we have to exorcize our own demons and come to terms with an impersonal universe. But the uniqueness of the present situation, which makes all misgivings ridiculous, is that the choice is now between common action to conserve human life and common inaction involving total annihilation. Some of us may prefer to buy time by more devious forms of rationalization. But those who are realistically aware of the imminence of total destruction will, to the degree of their awareness, be driven to action.

If the majority of people were sufficiently aware of the peril in which they stand, they would revolt and demand the elementary right of survival. Why do not the masses – here, in America, in Russia – revolt? The facts are available to them – facts provided by the nuclear scientists, by the military strategists, even by the politicians themselves. But people don't look these facts in the face: they prefer to look at football, or television, or just into vacancy.

The thought of personal death is difficult to grasp: the

thought of universal death is unthinkable. It is unthinkable because some mental censorship is at work. The aim of all active pacifists is to break this unconscious conspiracy of silence, to pierce this dark screen of mental obliquity. Propaganda is not enough: there must be action, and the only action that can have any effect is mass action.

Such action becomes disobedient when its scale interferes with the normal activities of the community – traffic, rights of way, communications. At present, those who are willing to commit acts of civil disobedience number tens of thousands and their passive resistance can still be dealt with by the normal strategy of the police. But tens of thousands will eventually become hundreds of thousands, and hundreds of thousands will become millions; and then the light will break through all the absurd conventions of international diplomacy and nuclear strategy. We shall recognize communists for what they are and communists will recognize us for what we are – all human beings, with the same desires and hopes, the same fears and anxieties, desperately anxious to find a *modus vivendi* – a means of living together in peace. Preventing the realization of those desires and hopes, as we see it, are certain conventions of political behaviour and international diplomacy. We flout such conventions, in the hope of uniting all men of goodwill, everywhere in the world.

II

Civil disobedience is the weapon of those who despair of justice.

We disobey the laws of the state because we believe that the state is lawless and cannot any longer protect our lives and liberties.

There is danger and difficulty in whatever course we adopt, but the greatest danger is to obey those who have led us to the edge of an abyss in which the world and all it holds of joy and beauty will perish for ever.

A MATTER OF LIFE

Transfixed in hideous enmity two giants face each other across the world, each armed with bombs that can annihilate everything that lives.

They hate each other because they obey the law of the jungle. They lust for absolute power, but to what end? Each says in order that mankind may be free, but by mankind they mean their own kind, communist or capitalist, and by freedom they mean the privilege of dominating the rest of the world. Their laws are the laws of pride and possession, of lust and avarice, and these laws we will disobey.

We too recognize the rule of law, but our law is the law of Humanity, which we also call the law of God. At this stage in history the human law and the civil law confront and contradict each other. Which law shall we obey, the human law that requires us to hold life in reverence and to live in peace, or the civil law which requires us to destroy – not merely to kill our enemies, those who oppose our will to power, but to kill the innocent and the defenceless, to destroy whole nations and even all human life?

There is no place for logic in this situation – no place for argument or debate. The deepest and most sacred instincts of mankind are evoked: the instincts that bid us live and love and aid one another.

One man is a Russian, another is an American. One is called a communist, the other is called a democrat. One is an atheist, or a Marxist, the other is a Buddhist, or a Christian. But what do these differences mean in a world threatened by total destruction?

Beyond these differences is the unity that makes us human—the unity of love and fear, the unity of flesh and blood, of hunger and satisfaction, of sorrow and joy, the unity of children lost in an indifferent universe. We are united in all that makes us human, divided in all that makes us subhuman and brutish.

There is a law that is the law of humanity, and that law we shall obey. There is another law that is the law of the jungle, and this law which our politicians call civil we shall disobey and destroy.

In civil disobedience all our liberties were born – freedom from the tyranny of kings and from the power of oligarchies, freedom from poverty and ignorance, freedom from slavery and imperialism – all these were won by men who had the courage to disobey the civil law, the will to resist injustice and evil. We are now faced by the final challenge. The greatest liberty is the liberty to live – just to live. For that liberty we must make the greatest sacrifices – our personal freedom for the sake of the freedom of mankind, if necessary our lives for the sake of life itself.

BERTRAND RUSSELL

Earl Russell was born in 1872. He was educated at Trinity College, Cambridge, where he qualified in mathematics and moral sciences. In 1949 he was given the Order of Merit and in 1950 the Nobel Prize for Literature. He has been a Fellow of the Royal Society since 1908 and has published many works on mathematics, philosophy and sociology. During his lifetime he has published a formidable range of works, including essays and novels.

THE Committee of 100, as your readers are aware, calls for non-violent civil disobedience on a large scale as a means of inducing the British Government (and others, we hope, in due course) to abandon nuclear weapons and the protection that they are supposed to afford. Many critics have objected that civil disobedience is immoral, at any rate where the government is democratic. It is my purpose to combat this view, not in general, but in the case of non-violent civil disobedience on behalf of certain aims advocated by the Committee of 100.

It is necessary to begin with some abstract principles of ethics. There are, broadly speaking, two types of ethical theory. One of these, which is exemplified in the Decalogue, lays down rules of conduct which are supposed to hold in all cases, regardless of the effects of obeying them. The other theory, while admitting that some rules of conduct are valid in a very great majority of cases, is prepared to consider the consequences of actions and to permit breaches of the rules where the consequences of obeying the rules are obviously undesirable. In practice, most people adopt the second point of view, and only appeal to the first in controversies with opponents.

Let us take a few examples. Suppose a physically powerful man, suffering from hydrophobia, was about to bite your children, and the only way of preventing him was to kill him. I think very few people would think you unjustified in adopting this method of saving your children's lives. Those who thought you justified would not deny that the prohibition of murder is *almost* always right. Probably they would go on to say that this particular sort of killing should not be called 'murder'. They would define 'murder' as 'unjustifiable homicide'. In that case, the precept that murder is wrong becomes a tautology, but the ethical question remains: 'What sort of killing is to be labelled as murder?' Or take, again, the commandment not to steal. Almost everybody would agree that in an immense majority of cases it is right to obey this commandment. But suppose you were a refugee, fleeing with your family from persecution, and you could not obtain food except by stealing. Most people would agree that you would be justified in stealing. The only exceptions would be those who approved of the tyranny from which you were trying to escape.

There have been many cases in history where the issue was not so clear. In the time of Pope Gregory VI, simony was rife in the Church. Pope Gregory VI, by means of simony, became Pope and did so in order to abolish simony. In this he was largely successful, and final success was achieved by his disciple and admirer, Pope Gregory VII, who was one of the most illustrious of Popes. I will not express an opinion on the conduct of Gregory VI, which has remained a controversial issue down to the present day.

The only rule, in all such doubtful cases, is to consider the consequences of the action in question. We must include among these consequences the bad effect of weakening respect for a rule which is usually right. But, even when this is taken into account, there will be cases where even the most generally acceptable rule of conduct should be broken.

So much for general theory. I will come now one step nearer to the moral problem with which we are concerned.

What is to be said about a rule enjoining respect for law? Let us first consider the arguments in favour of such a rule. Without law, a civilized community is impossible. Where there is general disrespect for the law, all kinds of evil consequences are sure to follow. A notable example was the failure of prohibition in America. In this case it became obvious that the only cure was a change in the law, since it was impossible to obtain general respect for the law as it stood. This view prevailed, in spite of the fact that those who broke the law were not actuated by what are called conscientious

motives. This case made it obvious that respect for
has two sides. If there is to be respect for the law
must be generally considered to be worthy of respe

The main argument in favour of respect for law is ...,
in disputes between two parties, it substitutes a neutral
authority for private bias which would be likely in the
absence of law. The force which the law can exert is, in
most such cases, irresistible, and therefore only has to be
invoked in the case of a minority of reckless criminals. The
net result is a community in which most people are peaceful.
These reasons for the reign of law are admitted in the great
majority of cases, except by anarchists. I have no wish to
dispute their validity save in exceptional circumstances.

There is one very large class of cases in which the law does
not have the merit of being impartial as between the disputants. This is when one of the disputants is the state. The
state makes the laws and, unless there is a very vigilant
public opinion in defence of justifiable liberties, the state will
make the law such as suits its own convenience, which may
not be what is for the public good. In the Nuremberg trials
war criminals were condemned for obeying the orders of the
state, though their condemnation was only possible after the
state in question had suffered military defeat. But it is noteworthy that the powers which defeated Germany all agreed
that failure to practise civil disobedience may deserve
punishment.

Those who find fault with the particular form of civil
disobedience which I am concerned to justify maintain that
breaches of the law, though they may be justified under a
despotic régime, can never be justified in a democracy. I
cannot see any validity whatever in this contention. There
are many ways in which nominally democratic governments
can fail to carry out principles which friends of democracy
should respect. Take, for example, the case of Ireland before
it achieved independence. Formally, the Irish had the same
democratic rights as the British. They could send represen-

tatives to Westminster and plead their case by all the received democratic processes. But, in spite of this, they were in a minority which, if they had confined themselves to legal methods, would have been permanent. They won their independence by breaking the law. If they had not broken it, they could not have won.

There are many other ways in which governments, which are nominally democratic, fail to be so. A great many questions are so complex that only a few experts can understand them. When the bank rate is raised or lowered, what proportion of the electorate can judge whether it was right to do so? And, if anyone who has no official position criticizes the action of the Bank of England, the only witnesses who can give authoritative evidence will be men responsible for what has been done, or closely connected with those who are responsible. Not only in questions of finance, but still more in military and diplomatic questions, there is in every civilized state a well-developed technique of concealment. If the government wishes some fact to remain unknown, almost all major organs of publicity will assist in concealment. In such cases it often happens that the truth can only be made known, if at all, by persistent and self-sacrificing efforts involving obloquy and perhaps disgrace. Sometimes, if the matter rouses sufficient passion, the truth comes to be known in the end. This happened, for example, in the Dreyfus Case. But where the matter is less sensational the ordinary voter is likely to be left permanently in ignorance.

For such reasons democracy, though much less liable to abuses than dictatorship, is by no means immune to abuses of power by those in authority or by corrupt interests. If valuable liberties are to be preserved there have to be people willing to criticize authority and even, on occasion, to disobey it.

Those who most loudly proclaim their respect for law are in many cases quite unwilling that the domain of law should extend to international relations. In relations between states the only law is still the law of the jungle. What decides a dispute is the question of which side can cause the greatest number of deaths to the other side. Those who do not accept this criterion are apt to be accused of lack of patriotism. This makes it impossible not to suspect that law is only valued where it already exists, and not as an alternative to war.

This brings me at last to the particular form of non-violent civil disobedience which is advocated and practised by the Committee of 100. Those who study nuclear weapons and the probable course of nuclear war are divided into two classes. There are, on the one hand, people employed by governments, and, on the other hand, unofficial people who are actuated by a realization of the dangers and catastrophes which are probable if governmental policies remain unchanged. There are a number of questions in dispute. I will mention a few of them. What is the likelihood of a nuclear war by accident? What is to be feared from fall-out? What proportion of the population is likely to survive an all-out nuclear war? On every one of these questions independent students find that official apologists and policy-makers give answers which, to an unbiased inquirer, appear grossly and murderously misleading. To make known to the general population what independent inquirers believe to be the true answers to these questions is a very difficult matter. Where the truth is difficult to ascertain there is a natural inclination to believe what official authorities assert. This is especially the case when what they assert enables people to dismiss uneasiness as needlessly alarmist. The major organs of publicity feel themselves part of the Establishment and are very reluctant to take a course which the Establishment will frown on. Long and frustrating experience has proved, to those among us who have endeavoured to make unpleasant facts known, that orthodox methods, alone, are insufficient. By means of civil disobedience a certain kind of publicity becomes possible. What we do is reported, though as far

A MATTER OF LIFE

as possible our reasons for what we do are not mentioned. The policy of suppressing our reasons, however, has only very partial success. Many people are roused to inquire into questions which they had been willing to ignore. Many people, especially among the young, come to share the opinion that governments, by means of lies and evasions, are luring whole populations to destruction. It seems not unlikely that, in the end, an irresistible popular movement of protest will compel governments to allow their subjects to continue to exist. On the basis of long experience, we are convinced that this object cannot be achieved by law-abiding methods alone. Speaking for myself, I regard this as the most important reason for adopting civil disobedience.

Another reason for endeavouring to spread knowledge about nuclear warfare is the extreme imminence of the peril. Legally legitimate methods of spreading this knowledge have been proved to be very slow, and we believe, on the basis of experience, that only such methods as we have adopted can spread the necessary knowledge before it is too late. As things stand, a nuclear war, probably by accident, may occur at any moment. Each day that passes without such a war is a matter of luck, and it cannot be expected that luck will hold indefinitely. Any day, at any hour, the whole population of Britain may perish. Strategists and negotiators play a leisurely game in which procrastination is one of the received methods. It is urgent that the populations of East and West compel both sides to realize that the time at their disposal is limited and that, while present methods continue, disaster is possible at any moment, and almost certain sooner or later.

There is, however, still another reason for employing non-violent civil disobedience which is very powerful and deserves respect. The programmes of mass extermination, upon which vast sums of public money are being spent, must fill every humane person with feelings of utter horror. The West is told that communism is wicked; the East is told that capitalism is wicked. Both sides deduce that the nations which favour either are to be 'obliterated', to use Khrushchev's word. I do not doubt that each side is right in thinking that a nuclear war would destroy the other side's 'ism', but each side is hopelessly mistaken if it thinks that a nuclear war could establish its own 'ism'. Nothing that either East or West desires can result from a nuclear war. If both sides could be made to understand this, it would become possible for both sides to realize that there can be no victory for either, but only total defeat for both. If this entirely obvious fact were publicly admitted in a joint statement by Khrushchev and Kennedy, a compromise method of coexistence could be negotiated giving each side quite obviously a thousand times more of what it wants than could be achieved by war. The utter uselessness of war, in the present age, is completely obvious except to those who have been so schooled in past traditions that they are incapable of thinking in terms of the world that we now have to live in. Those of us who protest against nuclear weapons and nuclear war cannot acquiesce in a world in which each man owes such freedom as remains to him to the capacity of his government to cause many hundreds of millions of deaths by pressing a button. This is to us an abomination, and rather than seem to acquiesce in it we are willing, if necessary, to become outcasts and to suffer whatever obloquy and whatever hardship may be involved in standing aloof from the governmental framework. This thing is a horror. It is something in the shadow of which nothing good can flourish. I am convinced that, on purely political grounds, our reasoned case is unanswerable. But, beyond all political considerations, there is the determination not to be an accomplice in the worst crime that human beings have ever contemplated. We are shocked, and rightly shocked, by Hitler's extermination of six million Jews, but the governments of East and West calmly contemplate the possibility of a massacre at least a hundred times greater than that perpetrated by Hitler. Those who realize the magnitude of this horror cannot even *seem* to acquiesce in the policies from which it springs. It is this feeling, much more than any political calculation, that gives fervour and strength to our movement, a kind of fervour and a kind of strength which, if a nuclear war does not soon end us all, will make our movement grow until it reaches the point where governments can no longer refuse to let mankind survive.

ALBERT SCHWEITZER

Dr Albert Schweitzer was born in Kayserberg, Upper Alsace, in 1875. He was awarded the Nobel Peace Prize in 1954, the Order of Merit in 1955 and holds four doctorates in music, theology, medicine, philosophy, and many honorary doctorates. He is perhaps best known as a missionary surgeon and founder of the hospital at Lambaréné in Equatorial Africa. He has published many books on philosophy and theology and is considered the definitive biographer of Bach.

IN the first half of the nineteenth century European philosophy and its chief exponent, Hegel (1770–1831), were concerned with the problem of culture as a whole, that is, with the culture of the individual, and with examining the nature of society. Philosophy aimed at making ethical culture based on humanitarian ideals a reality, and sought to promote the profoundest and noblest qualities in mankind.

In the second half of the nineteenth century the development and realization of culture follows two differing paths. Friedrich Nietzsche (1844–1900) was occupied with the problem of what man was to become according to his true nature. Karl Marx (1818–83), on the other hand, explored the means by which human society could be organized in order to make culture a reality in the most natural way.

As philosophy ceased to consider culture as the all-embracing problem, the ideal of ethical culture which had evolved over the centuries begins to disappear.

What contributions do these two new and growing modes of thought make towards the realization of culture?

Socialist thinking envisaged a society based on a collective pattern, which could be both practicable and worthwhile. However, this does not, in itself, represent the true ideal of culture. Culture presupposes an individual endowed with free will, who can fulfil himself in society.

The philosophy of the second half of the nineteenth century concerned with individual man did not succeed in arriving at a concept of ethical culture. Friedrich Nietzsche denies the ideal of ethical man. In its place he presents the ideal of the Superman, in whom the will for power replaces the will to do good. This hollow ideal, though couched in the most impressive language, stemmed from a man who was sick both in body and mind, and forced itself upon the thinking of that time. There may well have been personalities

A MATTER OF LIFE

who spoke out against Nietzsche. But the manner in which they did so was not forceful enough to be effective.

The course of events produced a situation where the concept of ethical culture was compelled to yield to the ideal of power. Tremendous power could now be displayed in the form of advanced weapons, and this impressed mankind. From the beginning of the twentieth century the range and explosive power of missiles increased immeasurably. There arose new means of extending the use and effect of these weapons. Ships were now at the mercy of shells launched from invisible submarines, and the construction of aircraft made it possible to attack cities from the air.

This put an end to all attempts at humanizing war, which had been undertaken in the name of morality by the Dutch jurist Hugo Grotius (1583–1645). The Red Cross, too, had worked with zeal towards this end since 1863 not without a certain success. These efforts rested on the assumption that war was restricted to those engaged in combat, and that the civilian population should be spared as far as possible. From the moment that not only warships, but all ships could be torpedoed from afar by submarines, and cities could be bombed from the air, it was no longer possible to make a distinction between combatants and civilians.

This frightful brutality was introduced into war without causing any public reaction or grief at the time. The significance of what had occurred was not fully appreciated. Without being aware of it, man had passed from the age of ethical culture and tremendous progress to an age which tolerated inhumanity.

The will for power was further encouraged by the turn of events. Towards the end of the second World War scientific research produced the means of manufacturing the atom bomb.

The possession of power through atomic weapons is in itself sinister indeed. The potential of the latest atomic weapons is so overwhelming that they can in effect no longer be used to wage war. They cannot be used to conquer territory, as this would not result in victory. Neither are they suitable for defence. They are weapons for surprise attack. They cannot be used to drive off the attacker, but only to counter-assault with assault.

Thus an atomic war would be a dubious undertaking, since the losses suffered from bombardment might be so great that ultimate victory would merely be the end of a catastrophe.

Maintaining superiority in atomic weapons is in itself a wretched and obscure problem. The established theory is that the East and the West should maintain an equal quantity of atomic weapons, so that peace is upheld by the balance of the deterrents on either side.

What is the real truth about this balance of deterrents?

If we were dealing here with fully developed weapons, given the will on either side, a lasting balance could be achieved, guaranteeing a meagre sort of peace. Atomic weapons are, however, continually being improved. Consequently both sides are engaged in an unending arms race, where neither side can know for certain whether it is ahead of the other or has fallen behind. A situation where both sides are rearming cannot ensure peace. The governments of both East and West are gradually awakening to this realization.

A further evil attending the rearmament of both sides consists in the fact that the manufacture of improved atomic weapons necessitates experimental explosions which provide information for further development.

Atomic tests give rise to the most singular circumstances – those of war damage incurred in time of peace. This takes the form of radioactive atoms released into the atmosphere in great quantities during the tests. These atoms drift over the earth in clouds, and over a period of years settle on the earth's surface. This results in radioactive pollution of the air, water and vegetation. This in turn affects man who is exposed to radioactivity. He drinks radioactive water and radioactive milk, which comes from cows that have been fed on radioactive grass or hay. Man eats fruit and vegetables that have become radioactive.

The radioactive atoms that enter our bodies in this way continually irradiate our organs from within, giving rise to grave diseases, which as a rule do not become evident until after a number of years. These are chiefly blood diseases and cancer.

Those who will be especially in danger from the radioactivity released during tests are our descendants. The male and female reproductive organs are particularly susceptible to radiation. The slightest amount can cause the direst consequences for any offspring. The effect does not manifest itself in the first generation, nor even in the second or third, but occurs from the fourth generation onwards. From then on we must accept the possibility of a very high incidence of deformities at birth.

In deciding to proceed with testing one must be aware of the mischief this will work on the future generations of mankind, and be prepared oneself to shoulder the intolerable responsibility for hundreds of thousands of deformed beings. This is a contingency that must not be disregarded.

Nuclear tests are thus a matter of the utmost gravity, and do not merely concern those nations performing them, but involve the whole of mankind. It is amazing that those nations, who are not engaged in testing, have not yet fully realized that they will be equally affected by this disaster which will unfold in future generations, and in view of this that they have not long since united to insist on the banning of tests. Lack of reflection is a fundamental characteristic of the behaviour of men and women in our time.

In September 1958 negotiations between East and West to end testing had reached the point where a positive outcome could be foreseen. This hope was only partially fulfilled. It was agreed that there should be no further atmospheric tests for the present, with America insisting on the right to continue with underground tests, since these did not result in radioactive pollution of the atmosphere and of the earth's surface.

In February 1960 France assumed the right to perform tests in the Sahara in order to be able to retaliate against possible atomic aggression. This met with remarkably mild protests from the West, as well as from India.

Since October 1961 we are now once again in the position where East and West are conducting numerous tests, which they need for the improvement of their atomic weapons. The moratorium of October 1958 is no longer in force. At this point the arms race is being pursued with unprecedented fervour.

Nevertheless, negotiations for a test ban treaty and for nuclear disarmament have been started once more, even though on the basis of previous attempts they would seem to be condemned to failure.

Yet they are conducted in all seriousness. Necessity dictates that one must persevere relentlessly, no matter how many previous failures there have been and however hopeless the outlook seems.

What is this necessity?

Atomic weapons have brought about an unexpected situation, where the will for power has become a will to renounce power! East and West alike cannot escape the knowledge that these overwhelming weapons of destruction make the old idea of war no longer feasible. They do not afford any conquest or victory in battle that could lead to an advantageous peace being imposed on the enemy. A war waged with overwhelming, perfected atomic weapons can only result in gruesome and senseless mutual annihilation.

Whether nuclear rearmament does produce the expected strengthening of defence remains doubtful. What does result is a growth of aggressive power on both sides without providing any power of defence.

A MATTER OF LIFE

The outcome of the existence of atomic weapons is, therefore, that the West stands in fear of being overrun by the East, while the East believes it must fear the same of the West.

Since the situation urgently calls for agreement on a test ban and for the abolition of atomic weapons, why is this not achieved?

The establishment of mutual trust is something spiritual, an ethical relationship between men or nations, characterized by truthfulness and a deeply felt responsibility. It guarantees that any promise given will be kept. Where trust cannot be taken for granted, agreements have no meaning. For they cannot be carried out.

The delegates in the negotiations for a test ban and for the abolition of nuclear weapons speak and act as representatives of their governments. If, in this capacity, they do not trust each other, how can they continue to confer together?

They are trying to find an acceptable substitute for trust, as the trust itself is lacking. This substitute for trust manifests itself in the inclusion in the treaty of measures providing for inspections, and even foresees the necessity for carrying out these inspections. The authority to enforce this is to be entrusted to a supra-national body. These basic guarantees are the subject of the negotiations for a test ban treaty and for the abolition of atomic weapons.

Should the miracle occur, as we all hope it will, that the urgency of the times will bring these negotiations to agreement, then much, but by no means all, will have been achieved. An understanding reached by agreement on a substitute for trust can only be a temporary thing. The guarantees it offers for peace, based on a test ban and on the abolition of atomic weapons, can only be temporary and relative rather than lasting and absolute. Governments can change and the production of atomic weapons and testing can be resumed.

The ultimate solution can only be enforced for all time if a spiritual element is introduced – if there is a surge of public opinion in the East and in the West condemning atomic weapons.

This can only be achieved if we turn away from the barbarian inhumanity we have embraced in our desire for power and return to the ideal of ethical culture, where earlier philosophy led us, and remain faithful to it and reflect on all its implications.

We must denounce atomic weapons, not only because they are to blame for the deplorable situation in which we find ourselves, but also more especially because they represent the basest inhumanity. By using them we, ourselves, would be guilty of the basest inhumanity, and thereby cease to be men. Only a repudiation of atomic weapons based on these principles can be permanent, and will secure the foundation stone of the ethical culture of the future.

MICHAEL SCOTT

The Rev. Michael Scott was born in 1907 and ordained in 1930. He worked in London until 1935 when he went to India. In 1939 he joined the R.A.F. in England and in 1943, when he was invalided out, he went to the St Alban's Coloured Mission in Johannesburg. Since 1947, when he was asked by the South West African tribes to be their spokesman at the United Nations, he has attended and been heard by the Trusteeship Council nearly every year. Since 1952 he has been Hon. Director of the Africa Bureau.

With the conventional weapons of the two most powerful groups of nations in the world facing one another at ground level, on either side of the Berlin wall; and with nuclear weapons of ever-increasing potential patrolling the ocean and circling the earth, the peoples of the world must face the illusion of our false beliefs.

First is the illusion of our belief in safety through the power of the deterrent – the capacity to utterly destroy our opponents. This belief, that human beings have clung to since the dawn of history and all through man's brave attempts to build a civilization, has now become a menace; the greatest and most dangerous illusion of all our false gods. The great advance in knowledge of the nature of the universe and the application of that knowledge through technology makes it possible today for one hundred and eighty million Americans to be destroyed at the same time as two hundred million Russians are being annihilated, and the rest of this planet perhaps made uninhabitable – or productive of monstrosities travestying the creative process. It may be that the belief that safety can be found in a balance of terror is part of the other nineteenth-century illusion that self-interest and ultimately state policy can, in the last resort, be enforced by material might and power.

If you believe that this is the last resort in the argument between conflicting social systems and ideas, then it means that you must be prepared to use it. You must be at least as ruthless as your enemies. If you find you are losing out in the hideous race to gain 'supremacy', you may have to be even more ruthless, or you must be willing and able to strike first with the ultimate weapons of destruction to prevent being struck first yourself – without possibility of recovery.

That is the policy in fact to which the British Government has committed us; namely the readiness to use nuclear weapons in reply to the conventional tank-guns that are sitting on the frontiers of East and West.

We are also allied to a country – America – which strongly believes its great mission in life is to destroy communism and that it is possible to do this by military might, by nuclear or other destructive power.

We are also allied at present to General de Gaulle and Dr Salazar, whose governments are responsible for the disgrace to Western civilization enacted in Angola and Algeria, and in the heart of Paris, where defenceless prisoners are being beaten to death.

I mention these unpleasant realities because they reveal to us our true self as a nation, as many people in Africa and Asia see us – ruled as we are by the present government.

We have been indoctrinated by Church and State to believe in violence as the ultimate political argument. Those who execrate godless materialism in fact believe not in God, or humanity, for practical purposes; but in weapons of mass-destruction as the final argument. If this is so, and we really believe that it can settle the great controversy between the so-called East and West that is keeping humanity in a state of perpetual hysteria, we shall one day be forced to use these weapons or have them used on our behalf.

There are, however, increasing numbers of people in Britain, young and old, men and women, of many different religions, beliefs and political parties, who do not believe any more that these nuclear weapons can be effectively used to decide the controversy between East and West, to maintain any secure balance of power, or to solve the ever-pressing problems of hunger and growth of population. These problems are part of the conflict between communism and non-communism and with every crisis become more and more inextricably bound up with it. So that what is happening in Africa, in Viet Nam, in Iran, tends to become more and more drawn in towards the conflict in Berlin between East Europe and West Europe.

MICHAEL SCOTT

There are more and more people in Britain, and in other countries, who are coming to believe that there is another way, and that Britain could – with another kind of leadership – herself begin to lead the world away from this frightful dilemma of mounting competition in death and destruction. While each side confronts the other with the most hideous and violent features of its system, striving for the lead in destructive potential and speed of delivery, there is advancing on them from the rear the great unsolved problems of our civilization. It is these which could precipitate them both over the brink, whose edge appears to be the goal of statesmanship, though the immediate occasion of war might be due to accident or design.

Visible resistance to the insanity of these illusions was seen at the Belgrade Conference of states struggling to assert their newly-won independence in a form of 'uncommitment', and it was there that many would have liked to see Britain, showing what she has to offer the world from her own hard-won experience, her constitutional history and her technological attainments – having herself renounced her role in NATO and the East-West dance of death.

In Britain there are many millions of people who, though not pacifists, do not believe that human beings can be terrorized into submission to this programme of universal death. The peoples of the world will not be coerced even with all the resources of modern states, to acquiesce in tyranny, or in the alternative, which is so often posed, namely the corruption of all those truths and ideals which humanity has struggled to uphold against all forms of terror in the past – and perhaps even against the balance of probabilities in nature. There are things which are of immortal value, of even more value to an individual's integrity, than safety or comfort in an 'affluent' society.

It may seem as though there is little else that a man can defend except his own integrity, and in this crisis of our time he is bewildered by the demise of the institutions and ideals which have inspired previous generations – the claims and counter-claims of rival systems of salvation; national and other group egoisms, pathetically posturing and posing in what today all conspire to recognize as the Emperor's clothes.

As mankind crosses the threshold of the nuclear age into an unknown future of immense possibilities for good or evil, neither religion nor science offers him any cohesive force; any universal inspiration capable of uniting what history, geography and economics have combined to set apart, yet now draw together in one contracting whole. But in the chaos of competing universalisms inherited from the past there begins to emerge a new conception of faith and order based upon uncertainty about many of the fundamentals of life and human aspirations. The inner conviction grows that in the realm of human intelligence, knowledge and conscience, values are attainable which may seem to have here and now little relevance in nature and the universe, as we are able to perceive it. But out of this realm it may be possible to fashion a new order of things – a new conception of human nature and society, with a quite different design in beauty and drama from that which has gone before, channelled as it has been through the old conceptions of church, nation and state, in which human life has been organized in the past. Such a faith will be found based upon a new tolerance, because of the very doubts and uncertainties which are valued as preserving to us a state of uncommitment and ignorance and willingness to learn, to venture further into the unknown and to accept none of the restraints the doctrines of God and of nature of the universe impose *a priori* upon the inquiring mind. Rather there will be a new-found humility which will recognize the inadequacy of any belief that I, in the small compass of time, space and history occupied by me, can claim to have, perceiving no more than a minute part of the whole pattern of creation.

Ironically therefore, our appeal in these hours (which

may seem to some like the last hours of man's time to build a civilization on this planet) goes out to the individual man, woman and child and to the masses of the peoples of the world collectively. For it is only we and they, here in this country, and in other countries, who can save ourselves and save the world. There is no other saviour who can save us if we will not act ourselves, individually and all together. Certainly Christ, even by the most orthodox claims that are made on his behalf, never claimed that redemption was inevitable or automatic, or even that it was 'once and for all' achieved on Calvary. Was not the essence of Christ's 'new way' – something which played so little part in the world of his time and in the history of his Church, but in his life was a unique attainment for the spirit of man – a way of passive resistance to wrongs that are consciously or unconsciously done, a way of civil disobedience, inasmuch as when judged by the highest tribunal of justice known to the world up to that time, he refused to plead? When, instigated by the agents of the vested interests in Church and State, he was accused by the people he sought to save of treason and blasphemy, he could say: 'Those who take the sword shall perish by the sword.' And through the mouth of his follower, Simone Weil, a German-Jewish girl, who died on a hunger strike: 'Those who refuse to take it up or lay it down shall perish on the cross.'

It had been in the extremity of such a death as his that the last word had come, signifying surely the greatest attainment of the spirit of man in any sphere of striving: 'Father, forgive them.' Not for the 'wrongs' they do – but because 'they know not what they do'.

History will grin, the cynic may say of us in the nuclear age, to think that this is the species for which Socrates and Jesus Christ expired, but it may well be that the last word is not with the cynics. At all events, we must continue the search for an acceptable criterion of human behaviour. Enough has been discovered to enable us to deem the quest worth continuing, the venture worth pursuing further – and at least preferable to the alternative of turning back to the past, of seeking refuge in some contemporary hysteria, or some illusion of security in reliance on the old gods of self-interest, national pride, organized violence and the moral bankruptcy, which in our day is signified by the ideals for which in the past human beings have died gloriously and ingloriously.

No; we have to fight. And we have to fight with non-violent weapons. Not because we have no other weapons, but because these non-violent weapons of civil disobedience, of non-co-operation with nonsense, are the only ones that are capable of winning the kind of conflict that confronts us.

Not that it is to be thought of only as a battle of ideas – the economic, social and political conflicts are real – but, just the same, there has to be a great exertion of effort on the part of masses of the people to assert reason and justice, without destroying in the process all that we are trying to create – not only in ourselves but in our opponents.

The aim of passive resistance – or civil disobedience – is to find a method of opposition which will not do violence to one's opponents' integrity or intelligence. In effect those who practise civil disobedience are saying: 'We offer non-violence against the things we so deeply disapprove. We are prepared to accept the consequences of breaking the law of the state which by popular consent (where it is a democracy) has been decreed. We are prepared to forgo our liberty in order to affirm our freedom from constraint by a law, or laws, we disapprove. By this means we appeal to the conscience of our fellow men, to consider whether we or they are right, in a world in which many of our preconceived ideas and cherished institutions have lost much of their meaning. We resort to this method because the overall power struggle is stultifying democracy, and causing a creeping paralysis of politics even in a democracy like Britain, where Parliament is now swayed more and more by the caucuses than by the power of persuasion and free discussion.'

In any case, for our part, rather than acquiesce in a policy, or a law, which we regard as disastrously wrong for our nation and the world, we are prepared to accept the penalty of the law, and we prefer to dissociate ourselves from it rather than remain at liberty.

We hope that through our efforts – and those of others we may be able to persuade – we shall make it impossible for the government to govern with this policy or law.

This is not anarchism – on the contrary, it is a method of opposition which only those who have a profound respect for society and for its laws in the ordinary course will adopt. Essentially, it is an appeal to a higher law or policy than that which the state is attempting to enforce, and it is curious that so much of the denunciation of civil disobedience has come from the leaders of institutional religion, who, impotent in the face of the moral challenge of the age, tend to impose their own limitations even on the Christ they preach.

We have to organize civil disobedience on a massive scale. Non-co-operation with policies and politicians on this side and the other side of the walls of Berlin, and everywhere else which separates humanity; which deifies massive organized coercion as an 'ideology', and the threat of death as an answer to the problems that confront us.

We must replace those old and tired men who are incapable of such an exertion with other statesmen who are competent to find for us some solutions to the problems of our time.

In England something of this new spirit has been manifested in the support given by many thousands to the passive resistance organized by the Committee of 100.

We have witnessed the spectacle – unseen before in this country, of thousands of people, old and young, sitting down on the pavements outside the Ministry of Defence in Whitehall, and in Trafalgar Square. They have been the object of scorn and ridicule by the press, by journalists from the extreme right to the extreme left, and by religious and secular literary journals. They have been denounced by church leaders and newspapers, including even Christian Action's *Newsletter* and the *Guardian*'s 'snivelling cant of the unilateralists'.

Strangely, few have questioned what really motivates these old people, young people, people of many different races and social backgrounds, in doing what they have been doing. 'Beatniks', exhibitionists, cranks, are the epithets used to dismiss their utter irrelevance to the situation. Yet, somewhere, it ought to be said – not because these people would wish for any tribute – that there is something of courage and imagination, something at least of value, whether in the young student or in the old lady who, for days before, spent the night hours wrestling in her mind and awoke early on the morning of the day appointed to go and mingle with the crowd, and to do something which nothing in heaven or earth would have induced her to do – and to go through with her decision, terrified as she is, surrounded by three thousand policemen, not knowing what the outcome of it all is going to be.

These people were not there because they liked the excitement, because they relished a term in prison – so all honour to them, to the correspondents who refrained from the easy laugh, the facile descriptions, and the temptations to deride. All honour to the policemen who, after ten hours of it, kept their sense of humour. More honour to those who, unlike some of the mitred and bowler-hatted ones, allowed themselves to think: 'What is really happening here?'

Perhaps the beginning of a great exertion by human beings to save themselves by that little light vouchsafed to them from a darkness that seems sometimes to be closing in on us.

HANS THIRRING

Professor Hans Thirring was born in Vienna in 1888. He studied physics and mathematics at the University of Vienna, where he took his doctor's degree in 1911. In 1921 he was appointed Professor of Physics and Director of the Institut für Theoretische Physik der Wiener Universität. Dismissed from his academic post in 1938 because of his opposition to Nazism, he began writing his book *Psychology of Human Relations*, containing the theory of mental perspective conceived when he was a student. Since 1958 he has been Professor Emeritus at Vienna University. In that year he also organized the third 'Pugwash Conference'.

SUGGESTIONS for educational measures to im͟͞p͞͞r͞͞o͞͞v͞͞e͞͞ ͟͞t͞͞h͞͞e͞͞
world's political climate are usually countered ͞͞b͞͞y͞͞ ͟͞t͞͞h͞͞e͞͞
remark that it is, anyway, impossible to change ͞͞h͞͞u͞͞m͞͞a͞͞n
nature, and that, in particular, congenital tendencies towards aggressive behaviour could not be eradicated by attempting persuasion on purely rational grounds. In order to substantiate the claim that it might be both sensible and practical to impress upon the rising generation the knowledge of psychological and historical facts, as will be discussed here, this claim should be preceded by the following acknowledgment:

For the sole reason of being regarded as civilized people, the population of civilized nations are now already prepared to accept many far-reaching restrictions in the development of their natural tendencies, and to forgo gratification of their vital impulses. However, in the instance of group-relations, especially in the case of the behaviour of one nation towards another, our education, hidebound by the traditions of a classical age, directed the awakening impulse of human ambitions in precisely the opposite direction to that of the individual.

Within the private sphere of our civilized society a 'pushing' person is hardly popular; people are considered to be well-bred and cultivated only if they respect certain conventions, giving precedence to others and behaving with courtesy and modesty. In addition, observance of the fifth commandment, 'Thou shalt not kill', is enforced by threats of dire punishment. In group-relations, however, the opposite has taken place in past ages. One's own country's *sacro egoismo* is considered a virtue; any willingness to achieve mutual understanding becomes a cowardly weakness and the fifth commandment is given short shrift. Anybody who kills a person for private reasons, or is an accomplice to murder, can expect life imprisonment. But the man who has other human beings slaughtered in their millions in the interests of imaginary ideals of a short-lived value is being immortalized on monuments and in history books his name appears in bold type.

Everyone is busily employed educating children to behave themselves and give an impression – at least on the surface – of being well-mannered. But when they reach a certain age they are allowed to see films and watch television performances where violence, viciousness and brutality are being extolled. Moreover, such tendencies do not remain limited to the shady side of present-day media of mass communications. Even famous artists, creators of sublime masterpieces, are prostituted by their glorification of mass murder in the pay of war-lords. In the Palace of Versailles, in Leningrad's Hermitage, in the Vatican Collection, no less than in any other museums of the world, one can wander through one hall after another where the walls are plastered with pictures of battles.

While allowing teachers of religion to preach Christian charity, a person who distinguishes himself by an utterly un-Christian cunning and sheer forcefulness in politics – occasionally also in business – wins general acclaim. Consequently, any stimulus to human ambitions in this particular connection, and also to the natural impulse to achieve self-esteem, must fail to arouse any tendencies to control violence, but actually encourages its use. Instead of applying moral discrimination one shows admiration, and there is a bonus offered for acts of violence.

As long as it is still tolerated that the powerful impetus of human ambitions should seek its objective by methods wholly identical with the primeval instincts of sheer force and cunning; as long as our divided social morals are prepared to put up with the idea that somebody could become a hero while yet remaining a beast, it is hardly surprising that in such an unequal fight nobler feelings and reason should suffer defeat.

Therefore, an education for peace, based upon these psychological facts, need not even consider any hopeless attempts at taming such all-powerful impulses. What matters here is the elimination – or perhaps better still the prevention – in future of an upsurge of ideas which in themselves are the products of a certain and distinctive training applied for centuries past which might have easily achieved results of a totally different character, if this training of human beings had been of a different nature.

By using appropriate methods of education we should be able to achieve a radical improvement throughout the world. A network of good schools and their teachers in every country, together with equally satisfactory educational reforms, should become infinitely more beneficial to humanity than nuclear energy and the so-called 'conquest of space'. In fact, more so than all the achievements of technical and scientific progress added together.

I used the short term 'training' for the process of shaping and establishing ideas and conceptions. This term is meant to cover the whole complex of influences upon young people in their homes, their studies at school and their reading, and might also be – and equally simply – covered by the word 'education'. To my mind this education should never be the 'governessy' type of training, e.g. a type perhaps necessary to teach young people ordinary good manners. Actually it should mainly consist of teaching enlightenment, and should be pedagogic in its aims only in so far as it provides the definition of certain opinions and the appreciation of values.

Consequently it would be utterly absurd to imagine that the *education for peace* could be carried out by somebody who, cane in hand, stands in the middle of a nursery or a form at school and separates the children who are fighting each other and then punishes them. A pugnacious child, once he is grown up, will of his own accord become interested in totally different matters than inciting international conflicts, provided the compulsory reading of war books, or his history lessons, do not force him to believe in false ideals – as took place during the Hitler period. The education of mankind to achieve greater maturity and to reach higher standards in order to withstand the dangers of the nuclear age should in no circumstances allow itself to be deterred from its task of frankly disclosing any mistakes made in the past, and of criticizing them.

This type of education would have to satisfy the following demands:

1. Lessons should be adapted to the intellectual level of the age group between fourteen and seventeen years of age (incidentally, greatly underestimated, for during this period in particular youth should become acquainted, wherever possible, with the main ideas and aspects of human society).
2. It is essential to give such young people the will and the necessary basic knowledge for a better understanding of their fellow creatures and of themselves.
3. They should be instilled with a sense of proportion enabling them to form more accurate opinions regarding the grades of human values and interests, and of their own responsibilities and duties in their proper order of importance.

The more an education of this nature tries to replace moral compulsions by inner convictions, the more effective and permanent it will be. In other words, certain facts of knowledge and understanding of basic importance, although easily intelligible, should be conveyed to a young person which are likely to shape his general conduct, and which in consequence will make it easier for him to adapt himself to life within the human community.

The following summary of the most important knowledge of this kind, at least in my opinion, differs from the preceding compilation in so far as it is merely in the nature of a list and is certainly not supposed to serve as an introduction to this subject for anybody who might not be acquainted with it. In an abstract formulation, condensed into one single sentence with reference to each item, the various categories of knowledge as enumerated in the following might not be fully understood by adolescents of only average intellect. On the other hand, each of these might be easily understood by using concrete examples and by going into slightly more detail. If these matters were attended to in a course of studies completely separated from the school's ordinary curriculum, the whole subject matter – of which the propositions mentioned in the following are a part – might perhaps require no more than twenty-five to thirty hours of tuition, representing only a very small fraction of the total number of lessons in the two upper forms of high school or public school.

At any rate, I am not considering this type of tuition on the lines of a separate subject at school, but mainly as a course of studies for teachers. Later on, after this preparatory study, it would be the teacher's task at school to give all his lessons in the true spirit of such a system of education. Within the curriculum of higher schools, for example, the suitable subjects would be philosophical propaedeutics, particularly psychology, and also biology, history and the history of literature.

I

Facts regarding the character and conduct of human beings of importance in respect of relations between individuals

1. Generally speaking, no human being should be regarded as either entirely good or entirely bad, nor as highly intelligent or totally dumb. Every man possesses hundreds of different qualities and facets to his character, evolved in totally varying degrees. In addition, he is subject to changes through development, maturity and increasing age, and

through the influence of changing environments. Unfortunately, there are no limits whatsoever if such changes show negative or downward tendencies (in the sense of deterioration through adverse influences), while improvements, although not impossible, are definitely limited in their upward trends. The extent of possible changes and the influence of their own conduct are usually greatly underestimated by people who see their partners as a given and unchangeable entity whose apparent wickedness causes them endless suffering.

2. In the case of civilized nations, individual differences of character, of spiritual and intellectual qualities, are infinitely greater (if it were possible to express such differences in figures one should perhaps call them a hundred or even a thousand times greater) than the differences between the respective values on average of one or another nation. Consequently to pass a general, wholesale judgment on a whole nation is usually a sign of lack of knowledge and education.

3. As Roger Williams points out in his works, this great individual difference is not confined to man's intellectual qualities and type of character, but includes certain psychological qualities – the manner in which his system reacts to various foods, drugs and medicines, and particularly his tastes in the abstract sense, and the way in which he reacts to emotional influences and to aesthetic impressions. Any excessive divergencies of taste are likely to cause friction in matrimonial life, as well as in any other type of partnership.

4. Human beings are born, quite irrespective of their congenital qualities, without a chance of choosing their nationality, and are brought up in one faith or another. Even their loyalties to one or another political party, or to ideological conceptions, are to a great extent determined by the environment of their upbringing, while a deliberate

choice in this respect remains confined to a minority only. Consequently the frequently heard judgment of a person's character merely based upon his relations with a certain national, religious, political or other distinctive group is bound to be wrong. Likewise the unqualified rejection – although frequently justified – of political or ideological conceptions should not lead to a summary rejection of all those who believe in these conceptions. Therefore it is necessary to keep an opinion of a person (who, as pointed out under (1), may possess any number of qualities, some of them good and others bad) strictly separate from any opinions on a political ideology (which might be utterly false and disastrous).

5. There are also considerable differences in the speed of the maturing process in individual cases which result frequently in a strongly marked discrepancy between the intellectual and the physical age of an individual. It is one of the disadvantages of our educational system (perhaps hardly avoidable in practice) that, while determining the final objectives of education, little attention should be paid either to the very considerable individual differences or to the strongly marked specific talents or absence of talents in one individual, or to the frequently occurring, very obvious discrepancies between the actual physical and intellectual age of an individual.

6. The above facts lead to a conclusion which constitutes one of the main and basic rulings of human conduct: do not regard your fellow creature as a given and unchangeable entity with good or bad characteristics, as something final and irrevocable, but as the product of a gradual evolution whose further development is in constant progress, as a person, usually capable of both friendly and unfriendly actions whose conduct might – under certain conditions – become influenced to a greater or lesser degree by your own conduct or actions.

A MATTER OF LIFE

II

Facts likely to further the understanding of group relations

Tensions within certain groups are usually caused or at least accompanied by the emergence of overrated ideas. Therefore it should be the task of education, both of medium and higher grades, to enlighten people at the earliest possible stage regarding the facts that might cause certain human aspects and values to be overrated.

1. At certain periods certain things appear to assume an exaggerated value and importance in the minds not only of individuals but of whole groups, certainly as having greater importance than their more composed consideration at a later date would prove.

2. A simple example of the factor that might cause such an overestimation of values is *frustration*. The broken doll, the toy taken away, the fickle lover, all these suddenly acquire an exaggerated value and importance. This overestimation, as a result of being denied, occurs in children and adults alike. But it remains limited to the subjective or personal criterion of individuals as far as abstract and concrete matters are concerned. However, there is also another factor which plays an important part, not only in the mind of an individual but also in the minds of larger collectives; intensive *concentration* upon one subject. This somehow results in increasing the space occupied by this subject in our minds. Only by constantly concentrating upon it does it become more interesting, more attractive and more valuable. By contrast, compared with the effects of *denial* causing only individual reactions – overrating through intensified concentration may act in a communicative manner and may spread and affect larger groups.

3. Here is an example of increased value as a result of increased concentration affecting the individual. Enthusiasm

for some sort of occupation – either some toy or some work – the mind utterly set on a task, be it useful or useless. The question of whether such an attitude of mind is desirable or undesirable largely depends upon the object of this over-rating. The attribution of increased value at any rate serves as a stimulus to the perseverance with which many a fruitful task is being carried out.

4. The following are examples of increased value as a result of increased concentration upon a matter by larger collectives. In this category belong all types of manifestations commonly called 'fashionable'. A term which is confined not only to garments but also to the arts, sports and intellectual or political movements. Although certain conceptions may play a role of major importance in the minds of the masses within a certain sphere of culture, and may remain important for a considerable time – occasionally for generations – all interest in them will sooner or later diminish.

5. Unscrupulous demagogues frequently misuse this technique of collective overrating of values to incite mass movements as an instrument of gaining power. Religious fanaticism, national quarrels, racial discrimination and artificially-fostered class hatreds are the examples of manifestations securing an impetus only partly from outside, while the method of a collective overrating of values sets the pace of the movement from the inside.

6. The psychological mechanism functions in such a manner that matters of real concern appear somehow considerably magnified, with the effect, in some cases, of restricting our whole intellectual field of vision to just these matters only. In ordinary life this makes people narrow-minded and pedantic, with all their interests centred obstinately on trivialities. However, with regard to group activities, this same psychological mechanism might cause a type of manifestation one could call 'foreground-perspec-

tive'. It consists of a restriction of our field of vision to matters which as immediate subject of our activities stand in the foreground of our interests. During discussions by official bodies one frequently observes that deliberations concerned with quite unimportant matters almost accidentally come to the notice of the participants in the debate, like matters of procedure, formalities, lesser questions of prestige, take an inordinate amount of time and work, with the result that discussions of really important matters are either given too little time or have to be postponed to meetings at a later date.

7. Regarding a further, specific and rather important effect of the same mechanism, the term 'inclination to play at things' had been suggested. What it means is that a medium used to achieve a certain object gradually becomes an end in itself, while the primary object is pushed into the background to such an extent that the person is no longer conscious of it.

8. Another cause of the use of false criteria in respect of the value and importance of human interests, activities, and conduct in general, lies in the fact that there exists a certain law of inertia which affects spiritual matters in a similar way as it affects concrete matter, and according to which things have the tendency to remain in a state of rest or uniform motion. The two following points are examples of this tendency to remain in a state of rest or of uniform motion.

9. It often happens that certain habitual actions and habitual thoughts and also certain fundamental views of the outside world had been fairly adequate in respect of one or the other person's relations with his surroundings at the time when they became established, but that they were further maintained at a time and in circumstances when such principles and habits were utterly out of place ('missed chance of adaptation').

To cling to youthful attitudes of behaviour when nearing

middle age – to stick to obsolete conceptions of honour (i.e. the custom of duelling and such searching questions as whether or not a person was a satisfactory opponent according to the rules), and more dangerous still, to keep to certain rules of thought in strategics at a time when the technical development of rockets and nuclear arms caused all assumptions and postulates of classical strategics to be thrown overboard, are obvious examples defined by the term 'missed adaptation'.

10. The condition of uniform motion caused by inertia leads to a phenomenon which might be called 'deteriorated aspirations'. It means that a reasonable action to obtain certain results, a disturbance of the mind or any impetus, once it starts really moving, shows the tendency to continue this motion on its own volition with a flywheel's steadiness and persistence, quite irrespective of whether or not the original goal had already been reached – or missed – utterly devoid of any sense until the damage is done.

III

Facts of a historical character

Regarding some of the manifestations of mass-psychology as quoted under II, historical facts provide the necessary evidence, i.e. regarding the collective overrating of values (II, 4) and the deterioration of aspirations (II, 10).

1. There is utter disproportion between the transiency of aims in global conflicts and the permanency of their effects.

2. Fanatical and militaristic movements, being extremist and intransigent, have frequently overreached themselves and ultimately obtained an effect utterly contrary to their original objective. By inciting wars some of the aggressive leaders of peoples set a ball rolling which they would have never touched had they known the effect of their actions.

3. Therefore the general conclusion of historical facts is the following: practically all nations experienced a ruler whose sphere of power exceeded the range of his wisdom and foresight. Consequently terrible crimes and mass exterminations obtained either totally negative results, or results utterly disproportionate in view of the expense in lives and capital. (As this phenomenon showed itself practically throughout the whole world and at all times, it may be stated as such without hurting the feelings of any particular nation, for, needless to say, this also includes the past history of one's own people. Despite the greatest admiration for the gallantry of war victims one should not shirk the criticism of those who incited the war.)

4. The traditional method of teaching history, as applied before 1914 in German-speaking countries, consisted of probably more than 95 per cent of the history of wars and of dynamic force, and even today devotes more than half of the available time to this subject. Despite strictest avoidance of any appreciation of values, the choice of subjects alone is bound to give pupils the wrong impression of the value and importance of various historical personalities. However, when one takes a longer view of these matters, the importance of all wars and all conquests, with their utterly ephemeral results, disappears, compared with the magnitude and permanence of the evolutionary changes in the lives of human beings through the influence of religious beliefs, of science and of social movements. The fact that we are now leading a totally different life from our forebears and are never again to revert to this mode of living has no relation whatsoever to events that once represented the main subject of the traditional teaching of history. Here, too, a rule, already previously mentioned, though differently worded, applies: major and permanent changes in the life of human society – and, therefore, history in the universal sense – are never achieved by people who believe themselves to be their originators, but by the creative spirit of mankind and

by the numberless decent people who really care for the spiritual and social welfare of their fellow creatures.

Postscript

All the work in the field of education can only be a part of a long-term programme. Under the best circumstances a decade or two will pass before an educational reform like that outlined here will be introduced in the schools. Another two decades will pass before the newly educated generation can advance into leading positions. This is no serious objection to the proposal in itself. It is never too late to build a better world.

But long before this build-up is accomplished the world could be destroyed for ever by a nuclear holocaust. Therefore education for peace should be accompanied by quicker working measures. What practical steps can be taken?

Abstention from work on nuclear weapons has been urged on all scientists. But this alone is not sufficient. Even if no more H-bombs were added to the arsenals of the big powers, the existing stock would suffice to destroy our civilization twice over. And even radical destruction of all existing nuclear weapons together with solemn and sincere renunciation of programmes to build new ones would not establish a satisfactory state of world affairs. For, as long as no radical change in human attitudes is accomplished, the abolition of nuclear arms would only serve to restore the situation as it existed at all times before World War II, when dictators like Napoleon or Hitler believed that a better-armed nation might boldly wage a war without risking its own destruction.

Hence the only safe solution is this. No more war at all – neither nuclear nor conventional.

Shall we therefore call for general disobedience of all armed forces? In spite of the almost universal desire for peace, the reaction of the majority of all people to such a call would be negative on account of an age-old indoctrination. People have always been taught that their own group is permanently threatened by wicked neighbours, and that it is only brave and unselfish readiness for defence, loyally obeyed by all its members, that can save the group from serfdom or destruction. Based on such assumptions the idea of the just war is upheld even among peace-loving people. The general feeling, as expressed in innumerable declarations, is: 'Although we hate wars and try our best to prevent their outbreak, we must be ready to defend ourselves lest we be wiped out.'

While, therefore, a substantial percentage of the population would reject the idea of disobedience in a supposedly defensive war, there might be a strong majority who would disobey in a war of aggression. The trouble is that under present circumstances, lacking a proper definition, each of the two conflicting partners might convince their subjects that aggression is what the other does. Even the brutal military attack on Poland in September 1939 was presented by Hitler to his credulous subjects as a defensive and repressive measure against the alleged oppression of the German-speaking minority in Poland.

As far back as 1930 the relatively liberal Soviet Foreign Minister Litvinov proposed a convention defining aggression in the League of Nations. The definition drafted then formed the basis of the London Pact of Non-Aggression which was ratified by the Soviet Union and twelve other States in 1933. A similar definition was also used in the Treaty of Mutual Assistance between the American States signed in Rio de Janeiro in 1947. In spite of this progress in limited areas, no universally acknowledged definition of aggression could ever be attained. Since 1950 a number of committee meetings has been held in the U.N. where experts have tried to draft such a definition, but no agreement has been reached. In a series of articles written between 1951 and 1956 I have tried to explain the difficulties and to suggest a practical solution – all in vain.

HANS THIRRING

In view of recent developments I am beginning to realize the remarkable fact that the most radical solution of the peace problem is, at the same time, the least Utopian today – general and complete disarmament.

This radical and definite step was long considered a Utopian ideal of dreamy pacifists and quixotic world reformers. The decisive change of minds among the world leaders (not yet among the herds themselves) was brought about by the threat of global nuclear annihilation.

In March 1961 the twelve Prime Ministers of the British Commonwealth convened in London and issued unanimously a declaration saying: 'Disarmament is the most important problem facing mankind today.'

In July 1961 Chancellor Adenauer, who is certainly free from any suspicion of dreamy pacifism, declared: 'What is the use of a peace treaty while Eastern and Western powers are highly armed – ever ready to strike and retaliate? The most important step today is general and controlled disarmament.'

And the official document of the U.S. Department of State (Publication No. 7277, released September 1961), which was put before the General Assembly of the United Nations, declared on page one:

First, there must be immediate disarmament action:

A strenuous and uninterrupted effort must be made towards the goal of general and complete disarmament: at the same time, it is important that specific measures be put into effect as soon as possible.

And the leader of the other political hemisphere, Mr Khrushchev, has not only staked his own personal prestige on the case of disarmament, but has also succeeded in making it the officially declared number one goal of foreign policy in the U.S.S.R. and all its satellites, except Albania.

In this world, in which the attitude of the most powerful

democratic leaders, and also dictators, towards the problem of war and peace has made a one hundred and eighty degree turn compared to Hitler's and Mussolini's position, the task before men of goodwill such as ourselves has also changed. Though we may disagree and feel tempted to disobey in matters of detail such as bomb testing, we should first of all unite in making an overwhelming majority of all people on earth obey the principles solemnly declared by their leaders – and also to compel these leaders to stand by their words.

In his letter to Macmillan of April 12, 1962, Khrushchev finished with a sentence that has been suppressed in nearly all reports. He said:

> If it is agreeable to you, I shall be ready to go any day, at any minute, to any place, in order to make a treaty on general and complete disarmament under strict international control. This would solve the problem of nuclear tests by itself because such tests would become senseless when according to the treaty all nuclear weapons will be destroyed.

Let us help the leaders of East and West to keep their promise by removing the obstacles caused by mistrust and misinformation.

(Translated by the author)

CARL-FRIEDRICH
VON WEIZSÄCKER

Freiherr Carl-Friedrich von Weizsäcker was born in Germany in 1912. Since 1957 he has been Professor of Philosophy at the University of Hamburg, and Director of the Philosophical Seminary. He was Gifford Lecturer at Glasgow University during 1959 – 61, and received the Max Planck medal in 1957. He was awarded the Goethe Prize in 1958.

THE scientist is shy of discussing publicly questions concerning public life. He has learned that he should only speak when he has found something new, that otherwise it behoves him to remain silent. If matters concerning public life are spoken of, it is impossible to avoid repeated reference to what is known to every informed listener. The scientist has learned that he should maintain with certainty only what he is able to prove. But the problems of public life are so complex that it is scarcely ever possible to provide proofs. Are we therefore to refrain from making statements concerning them? Statements made publicly are a form of political action. Yet there is at least one science where action is necessary without full possession of the truth, and that is medical science. A patient's sickness will not wait upon the doctor's scientifically worked-out solution of the problem. Risking error he must act in the half-light of approximate knowledge. In the same way the atomic physicist gropes in the half-light in the presence of the political, military and economic consequences of his discoveries. Perhaps, therefore, he will long remain silent about their consequences, indeed perhaps for too long. Yet the moment may come when he must speak. The moment may come when he will be thankful if asked to speak. And that is the position in which I find myself.

Let me refer to the most conspicuous political event of the year 1957 – undoubtedly the appearance of the first Soviet earth satellite, the first sputnik. The most astonishing and the most characteristic fact is that the greatest political event of 1957 was technical, and yet bringing no man either immediate technical advantage or disadvantage – this gyration of a tiny aluminium sphere in the almost air-free space above us. It was a political event on account of its reaction on the thoughts and susceptibilities of two thousand million people – on account, as we saw, of its psychological effect. This effect was perhaps different upon each one of us. May I be allowed to attempt to analyse this effect, and its causes, by asking myself what reaction the first sputnik has had upon my mind?

I am a scientist, I am a citizen of a Western country, and I try to be a Christian. These facts all play their part in the influence that the sputnik has had upon my mind.

As a scientist I greatly admired it, but was not greatly surprised. I believe that the majority of my colleagues throughout the world reacted in the same way. Therein, I think, we differed from the majority of our fellow beings. Most people, whether they experienced wonder or fear, were certainly greatly surprised. That must have been the result of inadequate information. Indeed, the knowledge possessed by the scientist only slowly percolates into public consciousness or, for that matter, into the consciousness of the politicians. Scientists had long announced artificial earth satellites as a means of research for the geophysical year 1958. The Russians were three months too early and above all projected much larger satellites than had been expected in the West. Hence we learned that their rocket-technique was some years ahead of that in the Western world. This fact had not been known to our scientists. But actually nothing had taken place beyond the mere ushering in of a state of affairs that would anyway have come in a few years' time – namely that not only could the West reduce the Soviet Union to a wilderness, but that the Soviet Union could do the same to the West. I must confess that for years my own thoughts, as well as those of many of my colleagues, had been shaped by the certainty that such a state of affairs would soon materialize. Hence we were not very surprised.

Before coming to the political significance of this event may I add a marginal observation of somewhat metaphysical flavour? From time to time it has been said, and not exclusively in Christian circles, that man has transgressed the limits set by the plan of creation. We have, it is true, been commanded to subdue the earth, but not the heavens. Thus expressed this idea seems to be wrong, but perhaps it manifests somewhat too specifically a justifiable terror on the part of man faced with his own handiwork. I should like to try more exactly to say what, to my mind, is wrong with it, and thereby be able to say more exactly what is justified in the terror expressed in this way.

In the first place we have no more made the heavens subject to ourselves than a boy propelling shot into the sea from a rifle makes the ocean his subject. But let us assume that it is the first step that counts. Soon, no doubt, the planets will technically be within our reach. Presumably, we shall find there no suitable conditions for man's existence: perhaps we shall be able to subdue them to no greater extent than we have, for instance, today subdued the North Pole. The fixed stars with their unknown planetary systems will perhaps remain for ever unreachable, perhaps not. However it seems to me a reasonable theological tenet to regard all stars that can be reached by our rockets, not as Heaven but as Earth, using the words Heaven and Earth in the biblical sense.

We shall have to admit that those who wrote the Bible did not think thus. For them the vault of Heaven above their heads was the Throne of God. Yet this vault was not first shattered by the sputnik. It was shattered by the whole astronomy of the seventeenth and eighteenth centuries; and a contributory factor was the spectral analysis of the nineteenth century which taught us that the stars consist of the same chemical elements as our own earth. Thus leading men of the West have long realized the similarity of Heaven with Earth. The sputnik is another of many examples showing that what man has been able to conceive correctly he will one day be able to do. We have for a long time possessed a map of the heavens: it will therefore not be

A MATTER OF LIFE

altogether surprising if one day we are able to adventure into this charted region.

But is not this a religious aid to help us more fully to understand the Bible in its essential and real sense? In Solomon's prayer (1 Kings viii. 23) we read that the heaven of heavens cannot contain God, and in St Luke's Gospel xvii. 20, 21 Jesus tells us that the Kingdom of God will come with no outward manifestation but is indeed in the midst of us or as the Lutherans as well as the Authorized Version (perhaps wrongly, yet with profundity) translate, 'the kingdom of God is within you'. Heaven and Hell are not to be found in the three dimensions of space but in another dimension to which we point the way when we say that they are to be found in the heart of man.

If that is true, are we still right in being afraid when faced with the technical achievement of the artificial satellite? I said just now that what man conceives he can also put into action; knowledge is power. Is man able to bear his own power? Knowing the natural causes of his death he early learnt, what the animal never can, to kill himself: the Church regards self-slaughter as a transgression. Only such actions are proscribed as are within the bounds of experience; suicide is a transgression because it is a possibility. The hour seems to be approaching when all mankind will be able to kill itself. Shall we be able to prevent this?

We should refrain from merely examining extremes; a glance at the extreme possibilities of our existence may dazzle us just as does a glance at a too glaring light. Man is not only able to conceive of his death and therefore bring it about, but also the transformation of a life that has been natural to him into a new life belonging to an artificial world. Shall we be able to bear the artificial world? Shall we be sufficiently wise to build it in such a way and to change ourselves in such a way that we shall be able to bear it? True, we are able to conquer hunger and cold as well as diminish the burden of labour. But can our nervous system bear continuous radio and the possibility of crossing the Atlantic in a night? The term managerial sickness has suddenly brought this problem into the open. Perhaps it is only a problem of acclimatization, although not an easy one. Let us consider it in world-dimensional setting; even those people who have not brought about this technical civilization are compelled either to accept it or else to perish, just as the Australian aborigines are being destroyed or the Empire of the Incas has vanished.

The psychological problem of war has also changed today. Formerly war was horrible because it had the power to turn a man into a wild beast; but today it is horrible because in addition he can destroy his fellows as he can destroy vermin. Our problem is not concerned with rage but with lack of feeling. The victory of the technical world over man's erstwhile nature sometimes reminds me of the fight of the dragon with the lion in Leonardo's drawing. Crouching with mighty paw, every sinew strained, the lion spits at his opponent above him; but with steely glance, unfeeling, and stronger, the dragon pounces upon him and is about to tear him in pieces.

Far be it from me to look upon the technical world with pessimism. But we must recognize the dimensions of the problems that it sets us. It is the problem of the grown-up man no longer protected like a child, who can only survive if he creates for himself the conditions of life. Personally, I believe that the spiritual foundations of the technical world are dependent upon Christianity. Belief in one God has robbed us of the many gods of which the heathen world was full. I believe it would be historically possible to trace in detail the progression from the heathen who lived in the world under the protection of and in fear of his deities, by way of the Christian who calls the world's almighty God his father, to the modern technician who of his own strength is able to transform the world; perhaps modern secularism is a

Christian heresy. However that is not the theme of my lecture today. We must now turn to politics.

The Western world's reaction to the sputnik was surprise, shock that sometimes bordered on panic. I have already remarked that many of us scientists were more surprised by the panic than by the sputnik. I trust I shall not be thought superior if I say that, as far as we are concerned, the period of panic was already behind us. We were alarmed when some years ago we realized that, at some not very far-off date, the total destruction of our homeland, perhaps the life and death of all of us, would lie in the hands of a man in the Kremlin. Our alarm could not therefore be increased when we arrived at the point that we had anticipated, and had imagined all informed people in the world had, too.

It may be objected that it was not in fact the rockets that alarmed the West but the advantage gained by the Russians. At this point I should like to make two observations. In the first place this alarm is merely the result of a long cultivated illusion. The West lulled itself into believing that it was ahead of the Soviet Union in the technique of heavy arms and had even allowed its policy to be determined by this illusion. Let us be thankful that it has woken up. Secondly, what we know about the inevitable development of technology has long convinced us, and does so today, that the development of even more powerful weapons will not lead to the superiority of one particular side, but to a stalemate. If the state has been reached where I am able, at will, to kill my opponent, it argues no great superiority on his part if in the meanwhile he can kill me five times over. David had no need for Goliath's strength or weapons; he needed nothing but a sling, a stone, and a steady hand. Our life today lies in the hands of the Moscow oligarchy. Presumably it is not interested in our death, but certainly in a policy of expansion behind which there nevertheless lurks the threat of recourse to arms at times of crisis. Thus it seems that the freedom of nations – freedom as we understand it in the West – is only guaranteed by the certainty that mortal blow will be answered with mortal blow.

That, however, is a precarious guarantee. It rests, for example, on a technical detail, that the blow cannot be so rapid or so absolute as to preclude a counter blow. To make sure of this, aeroplanes today continually circle in the air loaded with hydrogen bombs. I feel uncomfortable under this on principle. If we pursue to its logical conclusion the idea of protection by means of weapons which we do not dare to use if we wish to survive, it appears to be bluff. I once tried to formulate this as follows: these bombs safeguard peace and freedom provided they never fall; if they do fall scarcely anything will be left to safeguard. But they protect us just as ineffectively if everyone knows that they will never fall; then the opponent can act as if they did not exist. Hence we must be determined also to throw them, and that means that they really may one day fall.

Now, all this is no conclusive proof either that a third world war is inevitable or that weapons are useless, for my statement contains exaggerations. It is today still possible to threaten a third world war, for there is a chance of survival: presumably the majority of the inhabitants of the non-warring part of the world and at least a much shattered minority of the warring nations would survive it, even if it were waged with the full ferocity of all modern weapons. Furthermore, we must reckon with the possibility that a government, perhaps even a nation, would prefer certain extinction to political capitulation. And because this is so it will not always be easy to expose a pure bluff. I only wish to maintain that big weapons cannot guarantee our freedom or our lives.

Let us consider particulars. Suppose that it is exceedingly unlikely that a great war will be decided upon. Then we must admit that this is exactly the situation on which communism bases its hopes. According to its doctrine a world revolution will not achieve victory by means of a world war but by means of economic crises and internal political upheaval; and the supremacy of the achieved revolution will be guaranteed by means of domestic dictatorship. War in this struggle is regarded as dying capitalism's violent self-defence, and therefore the communist world must be armed against it; and it is for that very reason too that communism is passionately interested in its elimination. Personally I believe this computation to contain an error. To put it rather simply, I believe that communism, contrary to its doctrines, has a revolutionary opportunity only when the process of industrialization is too slow or where it has failed.

Hence Europe is today fairly immune to communism, but not Asia. And therefore I believe that the real battlefield, where will be decided the fate of freedom as we understand it, is today in the so-called underdeveloped regions of the world. It is there that our great opportunity lies, but I doubt whether we understand how to exploit it.

Unfortunately we have not only to examine the alternative between war on the one hand and peaceful friendly competition among engineers and ideas on the other. There is the application of force on a small scale. There is revolution, there is alliance with local nationalism, or armed pressure upon individual nations. The tension between East and West is not the only source of possible war in our world. The impossibility of a great war solves none of these problems; we are satisfied – perhaps wrongly – if we are successful in putting them into cold storage. Let us assume that the West is following no aggressive policy – for indeed, in contrast with fifty years ago, it is almost everywhere on the defensive – then all these tensions are a temptation for world communism to nibble away one Western position after another until none will hold. It is possible to lose the third world war without ever waging it.

I would like to divide the measures proposed for the avoidance of these dangers into three groups:

CARL-FRIEDRICH VON WEIZSÄCKER

a. Limitation in the use of weapons
b. Easing of local tensions
c. International organizations

a. Limitation in the use of weapons. The idea of not using all the weapons one possesses and could possess is not new. Poison gas has, on humane grounds, been forbidden. The temptation to use it in the second World War was lessened because it could not be a decisive factor. Strategically as well as politically the H-bomb has the reverse disadvantage of too great an effect. A policeman, it has been said, is worse off with an atom bomb, sometimes even with a hand-grenade, than with a rubber truncheon. In Korea, Indo-China, Algeria or Hungary it was easier to wage a war which was psychologically not unacceptable to the world because atomic weapons, of little strategic use in partisan encounters, were renounced. The theory of graduated deterrents attempts to define cases where so-called tactical atomic weapons, but not H-bombs, may be used for sharply defined ends in locally confined conflicts. It has also been suggested that in certain cases the threat may be made by declaring the intention to drop an H-bomb on a particular town whose civil population has been given a two weeks' warning. Finally, an international agreement was suggested whereby atomic weapons would only be used defensively. This would only work if we supplant the naming of an attacker, which is virtually impossible, by a voluntary undertaking in the event of hostilities to explode an atomic missile in home territory and not in that of the opponent.

All these are carefully considered suggestions deserving close examination. Some may be impossible in the form in which they have been suggested and yet contain principles which may be developed. I cannot, of course, attempt such an analysis in a single article. But, in general, it may be said of them that the administration of a correct measure of warning can perhaps more easily prevent a local war than one that is too severe, or indeed than none at all. Moreover they require a certain discipline of the imagination and an attempt at self-restraint in action, both so necessary today.

The weakness of these suggestions seems to me to be threefold. If a local war started with 'tactical' atomic weapons then the local devastation would not be much less than that of a global conflict, at least not in densely populated regions, as for example in Europe. Secondly, the guarantee against a shift into total war seems to me weak. Thirdly, it would be dangerous to allow such projects to lull us into forgetting that they leave the decisive problems of our world unsolved. In particular, I believe that a greater renunciation of national and imperial sovereignty than the mere limitation in the use of arms will be necessary.

b. Easing of local tensions. I should like to comment on the question of easing local tension by telling you something about discussions that took place last year in my own country, Germany. As you know, in April 1957 a group of atomic physicists to which I belong drew up a public declaration about atomic weapons. Perhaps it may interest you if I try to elucidate a little the political part of this declaration.

It first of all gives relevant information about the effects of those arms that are today usually called tactical and strategic atomic weapons. The political part of it runs as follows:

> We declare faith in a freedom such as the Western world today upholds against communism. We do not deny that the mutual fear of the hydrogen bomb contributes considerably towards the maintenance of peace throughout the whole world and of freedom throughout part of it. But we consider this means of ensuring peace and freedom as unreliable in the long run, and we consider the danger that would, in the event of breakdown, accrue to be fatal. We do not feel competent to make

CARL-FRIEDRICH VON WEIZSÄCKER

concrete suggestions towards a policy for the Great Powers. We believe that a small country like the Federal Republic can still best protect itself and can still most further world peace if it positively and voluntarily renounces the possession of atomic weapons of any kind. On no account is a signatory prepared to take any part whatever in the production, trial or use of atomic weapons.

I have already commented upon the opening sentences of this quotation; as regards the last sentence concerning our personal attitude I shall return to that. Let me now take the penultimate sentence, that which refers to our country. It suggests that she should (voluntarily, and positively) renounce atomic weapons. Particular care has been exercised in expression in so far as the validity of the suggestion is in question ('we believe ... *still* best ... *still* most likely'); whereas a note of certainty is adopted when it is a question of how the suggestion, if accepted, is to be carried out (voluntarily and positively). If it is right to renounce atomic weapons then let us not renounce them as if they were sour grapes. But is it right?

We were not arguing about the special position of Germany, important as that may perhaps have seemed to us, but about the fact that it is a small country. To what would it lead if eventually all small countries obtained atomic weapons? The state of affairs then to be expected has rightly been named atomic chaos. All the dangers inherent in present conditions would be magnified sevenfold. Thus our declaration had not a national but an international aim. Yet we are convinced that our beginning must be where our civic responsibility lay – in our own land.

Having made clear the international aim let me now speak of Germany's position in particular. It should be noted that our plan neither comprises nor excludes the neutralization of Germany nor the creation of a zone free from atomic weapons within a greater or smaller part of Europe. Those are questions of expediency and achievement. I only wish to emphasize that everything we have said is based upon the principle of absolute and unquestionable solidarity with the West. Not for one moment is it our aim to loosen Germany's ties with the Western world; it is our aim to ask the Western world whether a Germany free from atomic weapons cannot serve it better than one atomically armed. The strategic value of atomic weapons in German hands would, once long-distance rockets have been developed, be very ephemeral. If, on the other hand, the renunciation of these weapons, preferably within the framework of an international agreement, could be a factor in the loosening of European tensions, a small price would have been paid for a good thing. May I, in connection with this, mention the lectures of G. F. Kennan with whose analysis I so largely agree.

c. International organizations. The most important international organization of our day is the United Nations. However little we may think of its effectiveness, and with whatever good reasons, we should not on that account avoid efforts to set this house in order. Little included in the projects just mentioned can materialize as the result of one country's one-sided act or, indeed, that of the entire Western world. Definite settlement needs agreement.

If, for example, atomic chaos is to be avoided it is not enough that some countries make voluntary renunciations, while others do not. Hence an international agreement must be drawn up to regulate this question, otherwise it never will be. I even imagine that one day the world powers themselves, so as not to be dependent upon the no longer controllable reactions of third powers, may discover a strong common interest in such a settlement. In any case those countries that today have no atomic weapons would no doubt make a better contribution to their own and the

CARL-FRIEDRICH VON WEIZSÄCKER

common welfare if they sought to bring about such agreement rather than strive for possession of atomic weapons.

An agreement would presumably need an executive body to implement it. In this connection I should like to draw attention to the U.N. police as a possible important future factor.

And here I shall break off discussing the possibilities of practical conduct, fully aware that as far as experts are concerned I have contributed nothing new.

I will now ask you to step back a little from the scene where our thoughts have been moving and to regard it as a whole – as might perhaps a man from another planet. I believe that such a one visiting us in this decade would say: 'You are mad. You have discovered means to destroy yourselves and upon your free decision depends whether you will use them or not. But you act in such a manner that this decision is never made; instead you exploit the danger hovering over you to force from one another concessions of secondary importance. You see everything except what matters. Or worse; you do see it, yet take no relevant action. Your consciousness is split. You are mad. You are not illogical; on the contrary, you are very consistent and very deliberate But your logic is the logic of madness.'

I have spoken as a scientist, and as a citizen of the Western world to fellow citizens. Now I must try to speak as a Christian to fellow Christians. What can Christians do in the situation wherein the world finds itself? I should not care to force upon anyone an answer to this question, but I should like to tell you the answer that I personally cannot escape.

Christians spread the Gospel by living the Gospel. The heart of the message that Christ taught is the Sermon on the Mount: the course of his life led to the Cross. Is that relevant to our question?

The madness of which I have just spoken is no product of this decade of our century. The problem concerning atomic weapons is like a screen upon which our era projects the gigantically enlarged image of man's inner problem. I am convinced that, at least in the occidental world, Christians alone know a deep enough truth about man to be able to cure the madness. They are not listened to. And why? Because madness does not wish to listen – the demons resist being expelled. But why is it that we Christians have no power over them? Often enough, I am afraid, because we do not carry out what we say; in other words because we are ourselves in the power of the demons. The only answer that I know for the Christian to the atomic weapon is the Sermon on the Mount. And I do not say that lightly for it has taken me many years to convince myself of that.

Our theology of today has no binding answer to this question, and I believe it is possible to agree that it cannot provide one. The controversy between those Christians who defend war and those who renounce it is age-old. Whoever chooses either side rejects an important part of Christian tradition. Indeed, Christianity has devolved the decision of this problem upon the Last Judgment. In practice Christianity has recognized both combatant and non-combatant. To this latter group belong priests and monks, doctors and Red Cross men, women and children, as well as men who in war retain civilian employment. Christianity has differentiated between righteous and unrighteous wars, between a righteous and unrighteous manner of waging them. It has differentiated between the individual ethic which inclined towards the Sermon on the Mount and the ethic of political responsibility which dictated the protection of fellow men by means of weapons.

All this inspires respect where the effort is serious. I do not challenge it. But if I ask myself whether, after reading the New Testament, I can throw a hydrogen bomb, then I know that the answer is no. And if I may not throw it, then I cannot make it for another to throw. And if I cannot make it in order that it may be thrown, can I then make it in order that it may be used to threaten? Can I be certain that the matter would go no further? Can I bluff here? Or do I thereby deceive myself? That answer which is personally valid for myself I only knew after I was compelled to ponder what my attitude would be if the bombs were to be made in my own country. Decisions are as personal as that nowadays.

If, however, I am asked what I consider to be right for the Church, I must first of all answer negatively thus: I cannot believe that the Church can say yes to the use of the H-bomb. If she is not able to say no she will have to acknowledge her perplexity either openly or else by complete silence. Yet I believe that members of the Church can do themselves and the whole world service if upon quite definite presuppositions they openly say no. These presuppositions will emerge from my discussions of the following objections one of which is theoretical, the other practical:

1. There will always be wars, and the H-bomb is the war weapon of today.
2. If we renounce the H-bomb we thereby reject all effective military protection.

The first, the theoretical objection, seems to me false; the second, the practical, seems to me, however, to contain a measure of validity.

The first objection seems to me to be based upon inexact theology, inexact psychology and inexact historical judgment. It would be theologically exact to say that the imagination of man's heart is evil from his youth; that is, translated into modern idiom, there will always be discord and positive evil. In private spheres there will always be a measure of bloodshed, of murder and killing and we shall ever be stalked by the danger that powerful groups, even comprising nations, will be formed for the purpose of asserting a point of view by the shedding of blood. There will always be strife, perhaps with other and more morally repulsive means than recourse to arms; economic pressure, lies, possibly brain washings and terror. But strife will, according to the intellectual, social and technical circumstances, change the authorized ways and means it uses in order to guarantee success. Thus war between regional units using weapons is only one such way. Who would have dared during the Wars of the Roses to prophesy a time when Englishmen would not fight against Englishmen with weapons? When in the seventeenth century the Quakers refused to take part in war, it seemed as if they were thereby sowing what could not be repeated until after the Day of Judgment. In our days the contention based on reason that war does not pay has a more terrible validity than formerly. I presume that the Atomic Era will abolish resort to national and imperial war; otherwise atomic war will abolish the Atomic Era. Behind all projects, some of which I have discussed, there lies this thought. We should be nearer our goal if we knew better how to accomplish political ends without the means of national and imperial war. It is one of communism's strengths that its theory shows an understanding of this fact.

Let me make a comparison with slave emancipation. However deeply the spirit of Christianity is opposed to slavery and warfare the Church did not in the early days abolish either. For eighteen hundred years Christianity accepted slavery as part of world order. In the nineteenth century it became profitable to substitute for slaves machines served by paid labourers. And now that opportunity presented itself, a strong moral impulse was set in motion and slavery was abolished even in spite of existing economic opposition. It is indeed doubtful whether in all cases the slaves' condition was improved after the emancipation. Nevertheless, an age-old institution had outlived itself.

So I say that, in principle, it would be sensible to strive for the abolition of national and imperial war by prudent means; such attempts have a chance of success. Now here we come upon the much stronger practical objection that the H-bomb is the least suitable means for the purpose: the prospect of peace, the argument runs, rests upon the balancing of fears. If we are prepared to fight with our inadequate weapons, then war is more possible than if we could threaten with adequate weapons. If, the argument proceeds, we are in no manner prepared for counter action we should deliver ourselves, our fellow citizens, our children and our grandchildren to a new slavery.

I fully appreciate the strength of this point of view and give emphasis to it when I see that this is obviously the policy of the Soviet Union today: to undermine the strength of the West by exploiting the prevalent and understandable antipathy to atomic weapons. I should not have referred to the logic of madness had I thought the problem easily solved; the logic of madness is logic. By its very consequence it exposes the madness of its premisses; but he who seriously contests the premisses must appear mad to himself and to his fellow man. Let me put the counter-question: what would be our fate if no one were to remind us what would happen were we to carry out the threat, as threat, is intended to guard our freedom and our peace? Would slavery ever have been abolished if men had not dared to say it was wrong? But to say a thing so that it is heard is not done by words alone but by words that correspond to deeds. A silent refusal will change more in the world than a strident proclamation. Again, as a Christian, I ask myself: can I justify the assertion that there must be men who will do that and at the same time refuse to be one of them myself?

The problem would be simple if the Church were, as in the first two hundred years of her existence, a politically insignificant sect. Clearly it would be her duty to practise the Sermon on the Mount and nothing else. But since the time of Constantine she has had a direct part in political responsibility. Can the Church on account of this responsibility say yes to the H-bomb? I do not think she can, for by so doing she would betray a greater trust. Is she therefore to say no to the H-bomb? I do not think she can because she is spiritually not qualified; she is not prepared for it. It is unfair to suggest a course of action to an institution not capable of it. It seems to me right to tell the individual member of the Church that this is no justification for his personal inaction. It is only the necessity to make a decision which leads to that crisis in the heart of man without which no salutary action can be expected.

What do I mean when I say that the Church is not capable of saying no? I ask you to believe me that I utter this prompted by no personal feeling. It seems to me that the Church, like the world, is neither practically nor intellectually equal to the historical events of today. To be sure, no Christian can so much as dabble with historical development without realizing that it is a tissue of human decisions made either for good or for evil. But even if a man believes that God visits on us the sins of the fathers as well as our own, can he in the bitterness of his soul use this against his brother? No, he cannot, otherwise he will betray a part of what he has already understood. It is only in this sense, without bitterness and in a spirit of self-criticsm, that I now add what follows:

A Christian is in a difficult position in this world, although as citizen of a Christian country he realizes it less than if he were a member of a minority or subject to persecution. Conformity may be an act of love, usually it is a form of sloth. Bad conscience, the result of this sloth in each of us, is kept in abeyance by means of ideology. Ideology, as Marx has taught us, is abstract thinking, speaking, believing in order to act concretely in an opposite direction. If ideology is to fulfil its task it must be the offspring of the very highest intellectual level of those who hold it. On that account the Church has an admirable theology and with it partly blinds herself to the reality in the midst of which she exists.

Believing that atomic weapons will effectively protect our peace and our freedom is an ideology, a well-thought-out ideology containing strong elements of truth. Yet its ideological function is to cripple our wills. In wars of previous centuries man was compelled to look his enemy in the eye. Peace and freedom have never been effectively protected save by personal intervention. The H-bomb, as long as it remains in the arsenal, demands no personal sacrifice from us except financial. And, only to take this example to serve for many, the difference made upon a state's finances is that the money will be lacking to carry out an energetic policy of assistance in the underdeveloped regions.

Trust in the H-bomb prevents imagination from attempting an approach towards undogmatic possibilities of defending our way of life. How many people in our countries have concretely examined how far political aims can be attained by means of passive resistance? Certainly, in my country, hardly anyone knows the simple facts about Gandhi. It is easy to establish the fact that this mode of combat can only bring about a decisive victory in very special circumstances. Has it ever been used as argument against armies that wars are capable of being lost or of ending indecisively? If it is true that, in future, wars are unlikely to break out, if even only on account of the H-bomb, then passive resistance will in many cases remain the only possible method of fighting. What it requires, just as does a war with weapons, is a determined and disciplined cadre. Neither this possibility nor the far more conventional political methods that I have discussed have received sufficient examination.

Hence I do not think that the Church is, as an institution, in a position to suggest on a basis of political responsibility the renunciation of the H-bomb; she does not know, none of us knows, what such a suggestion would mean. But she would know as little if she defended the bomb. The necessity, however, of deciding ourselves may bring us to a salutary crisis that will at least smash a part of our ideology. It seems to me that those who have already experienced part of this crisis may be able to render their fellow men a service if

A MATTER OF LIFE

without pride, or bitterness, and without making too much noise, they dissociate themselves from all participation in whatever has to do with atomic weapons and, if need be, publicly stand by their renunciation.*

* This essay was originally delivered as the twenty-seventh Burge Memorial Lecture on April 15, 1958, and was published by the Student Movement Press.

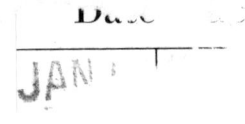